Implementing an Advanced Server Infrastructure Exam 70-414

Lab Manual

Patrick Regan

WILEY

SENIOR EDITOR Bryan Gambrel
EDITORIAL ASSISTANT Jessy Moor
TECHNICAL REVIEWERS Brian Svidergol
Ron Handlon
ASSOCIATE PRODUCTION MANAGER Joyce Poh

www.wiley.com/college/microsoft or
call the MOAC Toll-Free Number: 888-764-7001 (U.S. & Canada only)

ISBN 978-1-118-78946-9

Printed in the United States of America

BRIEF CONTENTS

CONTENTS

LAB 1
DESIGNING AN ADMINISTRATIVE MODEL

THIS LAB CONTAINS THE FOLLOWING EXERCISES AND ACTIVITIES:

Exercise 1.1	Planning an Administrative Model
Exercise 1.2	Installing the Windows Assessment and Deployment Kit
Exercise 1.3	Installing Configuration Manager
Exercise 1.4	Configuring Administrative Accounts
Lab Challenge	Designing an Administrative Model Project (Contoso Administrative Model)

BEFORE YOU BEGIN

The lab environment consists of student workstations connected to a local area network, along with a server that functions as the domain controller for a domain called contoso.com. The computers required for this lab are listed in Table 1-1.

Table 1-1
Computers required for Lab 1

Computer	***Operating System***	***Computer Name***
Server	Windows Server 2012 R2	RWDC01
Server	Windows Server 2012 R2	Server01
Server	Windows Server 2012 R2	Server03

In addition to the computers, you will also need the software listed in Table 1-2 to complete Lab 1.

Table 1-2
Software required for Lab 1

Software	***Location***
Windows Assessment and Deployment Kit for Windows 8.1	\\rwdc01\software
System Center 2012 R2 Configuration Manager	\\rwdc01\software
Lab 1 student worksheet	Lab01_worksheet.docx (provided by instructor)

Working with Lab Worksheets

Each lab in this manual requires that you answer questions, shoot screen shots, and perform other activities that you will document in a worksheet named for the lab, such as Lab01_worksheet.docx. You will find these worksheets on the book companion site. It is recommended that you use a USB flash drive to store your worksheets, so you can submit them to your instructor for review. As you perform the exercises in each lab, open the appropriate worksheet file, fill in the required information, and then save the file to your flash drive.

SCENARIO

After completing this lab, you will be able to:

- Design an administrative model
- Install the Windows Assessment and Deployment Kit
- Install System Center 2012 R2 Configuration Manager
- Configure the Configuration Manager network access account
- Configure administrative accounts

Estimated lab time: 235 minutes

Exercise 1.1	Planning an Administrative Model
Overview	In this written exercise, you will read the background information for the Contoso Corporation found in Appendix A. You will then read the information introduced in this lesson and answer the questions.
Mindset	By creating an administrative model, enterprise administrators decide who will be responsible for the various tasks involved in creating and maintaining the Active Directory infrastructure. By delegating these tasks, enterprise administrators delegate certain elements of their responsibility to their subordinates. This increases the efficiency of the administrative effort while reducing the overall cost.
Completion time	20 minutes

You were hired as a new senior administrator three months ago. Now that have had a chance to review the organization IT infrastructure, you are ready to design an administrative model that help lay the foundation for management of all systems and technology in the future.

Question 1	*For the Contoso Corporation Active Directory, what type of service management tasks do you foresee?*

Question 2	*For the Contoso Corporation Active Directory, what type of data management tasks do you foresee?*

Question 3	*For the Contoso Corporation servers, what type of service management tasks do you foresee?*

Question 4	*You are trying to determine if you should use a centralized, distributed, or mixed administrative model. Which model would you choose if you were an organization that that had a corporate office and 75 sites, each site having between 5 and 10 people?*

Question 5	*You are trying to determine if you should use a centralized, distributed, or mixed administrative model. Which model would you choose if you were an International organization with four large sites throughout the world, each site consisting of 10,000 to 15,000 people?*

Question 6	*For the Contoso Corporation servers, what type of data management tasks do you foresee?*

Question 7	*For the Contoso Corporation, what type of administrative model would you choose? Explain your choice.*

Question 8	*You have created a backup team that is responsible for backing up all data in the data center. What is the easiest way to assign user rights to those users?*

Question 9	*You decided to create a team that will manage the Exchange servers. The team will consist of 5 users. What is the best way to assign rights and permissions to the team?*

Question 10	*You have a distribution group that lists the SQL Administrators. You are trying to assign the rights and permissions to this group, but you cannot navigate to the group to assign those rights and permissions. What is the problem?*

Question 11	*The Contoso Corporation includes the Contoso.com domain and the support.contoso.com domain. Adatum Incorporated uses the Adatum.com domain. You have a file server that you want users from all three domains to access. How would you grant access to the file shares on the file server?*

Exercise 1.2	Installing the Windows Assessment and Deployment Kit (ADK)
Overview	In this exercise, you will install the Windows Assessment and Deployment Kit (ADK), which is a prerequisite to install System Center 2012 R2 Configuration Manager. Unlike previous courses, you will not be guided through each step. Instead, you must determine the best way to deploy the application based on the guidelines provided.
Mindset	The Windows Assessment and Deployment Kit (ADK) is a collection of tools and documentation designed to help IT professionals deploy Windows operating systems. Windows ADK is ideal for using with highly customized environments, because the tools in Windows ADK can be used to configure many deployment options.
Completion time	20 minutes

Install Windows ADK to Server01 with the following components:

- User State Migration Tool (USMT)
- Windows Deployment Tools
- Windows Preinstallation Environment

The installation files for the Windows ADK are located in the \\rwdc01\software\Windows Kits folder.

At the end of the installation, on the Welcome to the Windows Assessment and Deployment Kit for Windows 8.1 page, take a screen shot by pressing **Alt+Prt Scr** and then paste it into your Lab 1 worksheet file in the page provided by pressing **Ctrl+V**.

Exercise 1.3	Installing Configuration Manager
Overview	In this exercise, you will install the necessary prerequisites. You will then install Configuration Manager.
Mindset	The System Center 2012 R2 Configuration Manager allows you to manage your PCs and servers, keeping software up-to-date, deploying software, configuring settings, and applying security policies.
Completion time	80 minutes

1. On Server03, log on as **contoso\administrator** with the password of **Pa$$w0rd**.

2. Using Server Manager, click **Tools** > **Computer Management.**

3. Expand **Local Users and Groups** and then click **Groups.**

4. Double-click **Administrators.**

5. In the Administrators Properties dialog box, click **Add.**

6. In the Select Users, Computers, Services Accounts, or Groups dialog box, click the **Object Types** button.

7. In the Object Types dialog box, select **Computers** and then click **OK.**

8. To add the computer account of the server running Configuration Manager to the Administrators group on the SQL server, in the Enter the object names to select text box, type **Server01.**

9. Click **OK** to close the Administrators Properties dialog box.

10. Log on to Server01 as **contoso\administrator** with the password of **Pa$$w0rd**.

11. Click the **File Explorer** button on the Taskbar. When File Explorer opens, navigate to the **\\rwdc01\software** folder.

12. Double-click the Windows Server 2012 R2 ISO file,

Question 12	*What drive letter was assigned to the mounted ISO file?*

13. Using Server Manager, click **Manage** > **Add Roles and Features**.

14. In the Add Roles and Features Wizard, on the Before you begin page, click **Next**.

15. On the Select Installation type page, click **Next**.

16. On the Select destination server page, click **Next**.

17. On the Select server roles page, select Web Server (IIS). When you are prompted to add features, click the **Add Features** button. Click **Next**.

18. On the Select features page:

    - **.NET Framework 3.5 Features**

    - **.NET Framework 4.5 Features\ASP.NET 4.5**

- **Remote Differential Compression**
- **Background Intelligent Transfer Service (BITS) features**

If you are prompted to add additional features, click **Add Features**. When done, click **Next**.

19. On the Web Server role page, click **Next**.

20. On the Select role services page, select the following:

    - **Web Server\Common HTTP Features\WebDav Publishing**
    - **Web Server\Application Development\ASP.NET 3.5**
    - **Web Server\Application Development\ASP.NET 4.5**
    - **Management Tools\IIS 6 Management Compatibility\IIS 6 WMI Compatibility**

    If you are prompted to add additional features, click **Add Features**. When done, click **Next**.

21. On the Confirm installation selections page, since you have to install .NET Framework 3.5, you have to click the **Specify an alternate source path** and specify the **E:\Sources\SxS** path. Click **OK** and then click **Install.**

22. When the feature is installed, click **Close**.

23. Log on to RWDC01 as **contoso\administrator** with the password of **Pa$$w0rd**.

24. Using Server Manager, click **Tools** > **ADSI Edit**.

25. In the ADSI Edit console, right-click **ADSI Edit** and choose **Connect to**. The naming context should be Default naming context. Click **OK**.

26. In the ADSI Edit Console, double-click **Default Naming Context**, then double-click **DC=contoso, DC=com**. Right-click **CN=System** and choose **New** > **Object**.

27. In the Create Object dialog box, select **container** and then click **Next.**

28. In the Value text box, type **System Management** and then click **Next**.

29. Click **Finish**.

30. On RWDC01, using Server Manager, click **Tools** > **Active Directory Users and Computers.**

31. In the Active Directory Users and Computers console, click **View** > **Advanced Features**.

32. Expand the **System** node and then click **System Management**.

33. Right-click the **System Management** node and choose **Delegate Control**.

34. In the Delegation of Control Wizard, on the Welcome page, click **Next**.

35. On the Users or Groups page, click **Add**.

36. In the Select Users, Computers, or Groups dialog box, click **Object Types**. In the Object Types dialog box, select **Computers** and then click **OK**.

37. In the Enter the object names to select text box, type **Server01** and then click **OK**.

38. Back on the Users or Groups page, click **Next**.

39. On the Tasks to Delegate page, select **Create a custom task to delegate**. Click **Next**.

40. On the Active Directory Object Type page, click **Next**.

41. Ensure that **General**, **Property-specific** and **Creation/deletion of specific child objects** are selected. Under Permissions, select **Full Control**. Click **Next**.

42. Click **Finish**.

43. Back on Server01, using File Explorer, navigate to **rwdc01\software**.

44. If you have the System Center 2012 R2 Configuration Manager, double-click the **System Center 2012 R2 Configuration Manager** ISO. If you have a System Center 2012 R2 folder, double-click the **System Center 2012 R2** folder, then double-click the **SC2012_R2_SCCM_SCEP (Configuration Manager)** folder.

45. To extend the Active Directory schema, when the ISO file is mounted, open the \SMSSETUP\BIN\I386 folder and double-click the **extadsch.exe** application.

46. Go back to the root folder of the SCCM mounted drive and double-click the **Splash** HTML application.

47. In the Microsoft System Center 2012 R2 Configuration Manager splash screen, click **Install**.

48. On the Before You Begin page, click **Next**.

49. On the Available Setup Options page, click **Install a Configuration Manager primary site** and then click **Next**.

50. On the Product key page, select **Install the evaluation edition of this product**. Click **Next**.

51. On the Microsoft Software License Terms page, click **I accept these license terms** and then click **Next**.

52. On the Prerequisite license page, click **I accept these License Terms** for Microsoft SQL Server 2012 Express, Microsoft SQL Server 2012 Native Client, and Microsoft Silverlight. Click **Next**.

53. On the Prerequisite Downloads page, select **Use previously downloaded files**, Then in the Path text box, type **\\rwdc01\software\ConfMgrDownload** and then click **Next**.

54. On the Server Language Selections page, click **Next**.

55. On the Client Language Selection page, click **Next**.

56. On the Site and Installation Settings page, answer the following question and then type the following:

    Site code: **001**

    Site name: **Corporate**

Question 13	*What is the path to the installation folder?*

57. Click **Next**.

58. On the Primary Site Installation page, select **Install the primary site as a stand-alone site**. Click **Next**.

59. When you are prompted to continue, click **Yes**.

60. On the Database Information page, in the SQL Server name (FQDN): text box, type **Server03.contoso.com**.

Question 14	*What is the database name?*

61. Click **Next**.

62. On the Database information page, click **Next**.

63. On the SMS Provider Settings page, click **Next**.

64. On the Client Computer Communication Settings page, select **Configure the communication method on each site system role** and then click **Next**.

65. On the Site System Roles page, Install a management point and install a distribution point is selected. Click **Next**.

66. On the Customer Experience Improvement Program page, select **I don't want to join the program at this time**. Click **Next**.

67. On the Settings Summary page, click **Next**.

68. If any prerequisite is missing, the SCCM informs you before it starts the installation. Fix all prerequisites. When done, click **Begin install**.

69. When the installation is complete, take a screenshot by pressing **Alt+Prt Scr** and then paste it into your Lab 1 worksheet file provided by pressing **Ctrl+V**.

70. When the installation is complete, click **Close**.

71. Close the Microsoft System Center 2012 R2 Configuration Manager splash screen.

72. Click the **Start** button, click **All Programs**, and then click **Configuration Manager**.

Stay logged into Server01 for the next exercise.

Exercise 1.4	Configuring Administrative Accounts
Overview	In this exercise, you will configure the network access account and the administrative accounts in Configuration Manager.
Mindset	System Center uses Run As accounts to perform certain tasks or to access certain systems. The Network Access Account that you choose to use should have the minimum appropriate permissions for the software distribution or operating system deployment content it needs to access. In addition, Configuration Manager uses security roles to grant permissions to users based on their respective roles.
Completion time	25 minutes

1. Log on to the RWDC01 as **contoso\corporation** with the password of **Pa$$w0rd**.

2. Using Server Manager, open the **Active Directory Users and Computers** console.

3. In the Active Directory Users and Computers console, expand **contoso.com** and then click the **Users** node.

4. Right-click the **Users** node and choose **New > User**.

5. In the New Object – User dialog box, enter the following information and then click **Next**:

   First name: **John**

   Last name: **Smith**

   User logon name: **JSmith**

6. For the Password and Confirm password text boxes, type **Pa$$w0rd**.

7. Select the password never expires. In the Active Directory Domain Services dialog box, click **OK**. Click **Next**.

8. Click **Finish**.

9. On Server01, click the **Start** button, click the **Show All Programs** down arrow, and then click the **Configuration Manager Console** under the Microsoft System Center 2012 R2 section.

10. In the Configuration Manager console, in the navigation pane (bottom-left pane), click **Administration**.

11. In the Administration workspace, expand **Site Configuration** and then click the **Sites** node.

12. In the results pane, right-click the **001 – Corporate** site, choose **Configure Site Components**, and then click **Software Distribution**.

13. In the Software Distribution Component Properties dialog box, click the **Network Access Account** tab.

14. Click to select **Specify the account that accesses network locations** and then click the **Set** button (the button showing the yellow sun). Click **New Account**.

15. In the Windows User Account dialog box, in the User name text box, type **contoso\administrator**. In the Password and Confirm password text boxes, type **Pa$$W0rd**.

16. Take a screenshot by pressing **Alt+Prt Scr** and then paste it into your Lab 1 worksheet file provided by pressing **Ctrl+V**.

17. Click **OK** to close the windows User Account dialog box.

18. Click **OK** to close the Software Distribution Component Properties dialog box.

19. In the Administration workspace, expand the **Security** node. Then click the **Security Roles** node and double-click **Application Administrator**.

20. In the Application Administrator Properties dialog box, click the **Permissions** tab.

21. Expand the **Application** node.

Question 15	*What permissions are assigned to the Application security role?*

22. Click **OK** to close the Application Administrator Properties dialog box.

23. Under the Security node, click **Administrative Users**.

24. On the Home tab, click **Add User or Group**.

25. In the Add User or Group dialog box, click **Browse**.

26. In the Select user, Computer, or Group dialog box, in the Enter the object name to select text box, type **jsmith**. Click **OK**.

27. Click the **Add** button. In the Add Security Role dialog box, select the **Application Administrator**. Click **OK**.

28. Click **OK** to close the Add User or Group dialog box.

29. When the installation is complete, take a screenshot by pressing **Alt+Prt Scr** and then paste it into your Lab 1 worksheet file provided by pressing **Ctrl+V**.

    You can log out of RWDC01, Server01, and Server03.

Lab Challenge	Designing an Administrative Model Project (Contoso Administrative Model)
Overview	You are an administrator for the Contoso Corporation, which produces smart devices for the home. Read Appendix A for background information about the company and then read the information presented in this exercise.
Mindset	Over the past eight years, your company has significantly grown. The surprise growth has caused many of the company policies and guidelines to be outdated. Therefore, you are tasked with updating these policies and guidelines. You've consulted with members from various teams and you are now ready to design an administrative model that will be used throughout your company.
Completion time	90 minutes

The policy and guidelines will be used with all of the primary services across your company. Therefore, you need to determine the best administrative model to manage your services. You also need to highlight the primary services and apply the model to those services. Be sure to include how you would assign and delegate user rights and permission.

Create a proposal that includes the following sections:

- Purpose of Project
- Requirements of the Project
- Proposed Solution

When writing the proposal, make sure to explain the reasoning behind your choices.

End of lab.

LAB 2
DESIGNING A MONITORING STRATEGY

THIS LAB CONTAINS THE FOLLOWING EXERCISES AND ACTIVITIES:

Exercise 2.1	Planning a Monitoring Strategy
Exercise 2.2	Installing Operations Manager
Exercise 2.3	Discovering a System and Installing an Agent
Exercise 2.4	Installing Management Packs
Lab Challenge	Designing Operations Manager Deployment (Operations Manager Deployment Project)

BEFORE YOU BEGIN

The lab environment consists of student workstations connected to a local area network, along with a server that functions as the domain controller for a domain called contoso.com. The computers required for this lab are listed in Table 2-1.

Table 2-1
Computers required for Lab 2

Computer	*Operating System*	*Computer Name*
Server	Windows Server 2012 R2	RWDC01
Server	Windows Server 2012 R2	Server02
Server	Windows Server 2012 R2	Server03

In addition to the computers, you will also need the software listed in Table 2-2 to complete Lab 2.

Table 2-2
Software required for Lab 2

Software	*Location*
Windows Server 2012 R2 installation disk	\\rwdc01\software
System Center 2012 Operations Manager Installation disk/files	\\rwdc01\software
Microsoft Report Viewer 2012 Runtime (Report Viewer controls)	\\rwdc01\software
Microsoft System CLR Types for Microsoft SQL Server 2012	\\rwdc01\software
Management packs for SQL Server 2005, 2008, 2012, Virtual Machine Manager 2012 R2, Active Directory Certificate Services 2012, Internet Information Services 2003, Internet Information Services 2008, Windows Server 2003, Windows Server 2008, Windows Server 2012, and Windows Server 2012 R2.	\\rwdc01\software
Lab 2 student worksheet	Lab02_worksheet.docx (provided by instructor)

Working with Lab Worksheets

Each lab in this manual requires that you answer questions, shoot screen shots, and perform other activities that you will document in a worksheet named for the lab, such as Lab02_worksheet.docx. You will find these worksheets on the book companion site. It is recommended that you use a USB flash drive to store your worksheets, so you can submit them to your instructor for review. As you perform the exercises in each lab, open the appropriate worksheet file, fill in the required information, and then save the file to your flash drive.

SCENARIO

After completing this lab, you will be able to:

- Plan and design a monitoring strategy
- Install System Center 2012 R2 Operations Manager
- Add clients to Operations Manager
- Install management packs

Estimated lab time: 190 minutes

Exercise 2.1	Planning a Monitoring Strategy
Overview	In this written exercise, you will read the background information for the Contoso Corporation found in Appendix A 70-414. You will then read the information introduced in this lesson and answer the questions.
Mindset	Larger organizations might have hundreds—or even thousands—of servers, each designed to provide essential services. When a server goes down, employees cannot perform their jobs, products cannot reach consumers, and so on. Time is money, so you want to know immediately if a server goes down. Even better, you want to be informed if a server is about to fail so you can take corrective action before it fails or you can remediate the failure as quickly as possible.
Completion time	20 minutes

As an administrator of the Contoso Corporation, you need to develop a monitoring strategy for the corporation so that you can be notified when a system goes down and hopefully be giving a warning of systems that are about to go down. You will also need to look at performance trends so that you know when it is time to upgrade or replace a system.

Question 1	*You are working with the corporate help desk on a problem where some machines become slow. Which tool can you show to the help desk personnel to look at memory and processor utilization?*

Question 2	*You have several users who are having connectivity problems from time to time. What is the best way to look at the system logs without interrupting the users?*

Question 3	*You have 5 domain controllers that you want to monitor for errors and unavailability. What should you do?*

Question 4	*You currently have approximately 30 servers that you need to monitor, including looking at processor, memory, and disk utilization over the past 30 days. Which tool or program should you use to monitor these servers?*

Question 5	*You have 2,400 servers that you want to monitor with Operations Manager. How many management servers do you need?*

Question 6	*You have several folders where important files have disappeared. Unfortunately, you are not sure when they got deleted. It could have happened any time over the last 2 months. What program or tool should you use to help you monitor these folders?*

Question 7	*You have several consultants and you need to show when they logged onto the network. Which tool should you use to show their logins over the last 30 days?*

Question 8	*You just created a new external website and you need to be notified immediately if the site becomes unavailable to Internet users. What should you do?*

Exercise 2.2	Installing Operations Manager
Overview	In this exercise, you will install Operations Manager on Server02, which will use the Microsoft SQL Server installed on Server03.
Mindset	System Center 2012 R2 Operations Manager is the part of the System Center suite that is the primary tool for monitoring an enterprise environment. You can monitor multiple computers, devices, services, and applications using the Operations Manager console
Completion time	60 minutes

1. On Server02, log in as **contoso\administrator** with the password of **Pa$$w0rd**.

2. Click the **File Explorer** button on the Taskbar. When File Explorer opens, navigate to the **\\rwdc01\software** folder.

3. Double-click the Windows Server 2012 R2 ISO file,

Question 9	*Which drive letter was assigned to the mounted ISO file?*

4. Using **Server Manager**, click **Manage** > **Add Roles and Features**.

5. In the Add Roles and Features Wizard, on the Before you begin page, click **Next**.

6. On the Select Installation type page, click **Next**.

7. On the Select destination server page, click **Next**.

8. On the Select server roles page, select **Web Server (IIS)**. When you are prompted to add features, click the **Add Features** button. Click **Next**.

9. On the Select features page, select:

   - **.NET Framework 4.5 Features\ASP.NET 4.5**
   - **.NET Framework 4.5\WCF Services\HTTP Activation**

   If you are prompted to add additional features, click **Add Features**. When done, click **Next**.

10. On the Web Server role page, click **Next**.

11. On the Select role services page, select the following:

   - **Web Server\Application Development\ASP.NET 3.5**
   - **Web Server\Application Development\ASP.NET 4.5**
   - **Web Server\Health and Diagnostics\Request Monitor**
   - **Web Server\Security\Windows Authentication**
   - **Management Tools\IIS 6 Management Compatibility\IIS 6 Metabase Compatibility**

   If you are prompted to add additional features, click **Add Features**. When done, click **Next**.

12. On the Confirm installation selections page, since you have to install .NET Framework 3.5, you have to elect the **Specify an alternate source path**, specify the **E:\Sources\SxS** path, and click **OK**. Then click **Install.**

13. When the features are installed, click **Close**.

14. Open **File Explorer** and open the **\\rwdc01\software** folder.

15. Double-click the **SQLSysClrTypes** application. If you are prompted to run the file, click **Run**.

16. When the Microsoft CLR Types for SQL Server 2012 Setup wizard opens, click **Next**.

17. On the License Agreement page, select **I accept the terms in the license agreement** and click **Next**.

18. On the Ready to Install the Program page, click **Install**.

19. When the installation is complete, click **Finish**.

20. Double-click the **ReportViewer** application. If you are prompted to run the file, click **Run**.

21. When the Microsoft Report Viewer 2012 Runtime wizard opens, click **Next**.

22. On the License Agreement page, select **I accept the terms in the license agreement** and click **Next**.

23. On the Ready to Install the Program page, click **Install**.

24. When the installation is complete, click **Finish**.

25. To start the Operations Manager installation program, perform one of the following:

    a. If you have the System Center 2012 R2 Operations Manage ISO, double-click the System Center 2012 R2 Operations Manager ISO file.

    b. If you have a System Center 2012 R2 folder, double-click the **System Center 2012 R2** folder and then double-click the **SC2012_R2-SCOM** application. When you are prompted to run this file, click **Run**. When the Welcome to the SC2012 R2 SCOM Setup Wizard opens, click **Next**. On the Select Destination Location page, click **Next**. Click **Extract**. Click **Finish**. Then navigate to **\\rwdc01\software\SC2012 R2 SCOM** folder.

26. Double-click the **Setup** application.

27. When the Operations Manager window opens, click **Install**.

28. In the Operations Manager Setup Wizard, on the Select features to install page, select **Management server, Operations console**, and **Web console**. Click **Next**.

29. On the Select installation location page, click **Next**.

30. On the Prerequisites page, click **Next**.

31. On the Proceed with Setup page, click **Next**.

32. On the Specify an installation option page, Create the first Management server in a new management group is already selected. In the Management group name, type **OperationsManager** and click **Next**.

33. On the Please read the license terms page, select, **I have read, understood, and agree with the license terms** option, and click **Next**.

34. On the Configure the operational database page, in the Server name and instance name, type **Server03**. Click **Next**.

35. On the Configure the data warehouse database page, in the Server name and instance name text box, type **Server03**. Click **Next**.

36. On the Specify a web site for use with the Web console page, the Default Web Site is already selected. Click **Next**.

Question 10	*What is the name and port used by the Default Web Site?*

37. On the Select an authentication mode for use with the Web console, click **Next.**

38. On the Configure Operations Manager accounts page, for the Management server action account, in the Domain\Username text box, type **contoso\administrator**. In the Password text box, type **Pa$$w0rd.**

39. For the Data Reader account and Data Writer account Domain\User Name and Password, configure **contoso\administrator** and **Pa$$w0rd**. Click **Next**. If a warning displays concerning the use of a domain admin account, click **OK**.

40. On the Help improve Operations Manager page, select **No, I am not willing to participate** for all sections. Click **Next**.

41. On the Microsoft Update, select **Off** and click **Next**.

42. On the Installation Summary page, click **Install**.

43. When the installation is complete, click **Close**. The Operations Manager console opens.

44. Take a screen shot of the Operations Manager console by pressing **Alt+Prt Scr** and then paste it into your Lab 2 worksheet file in the page provided by pressing **Ctrl+V**.

Leave the Operations Manager console open for the next exercise.

Exercise 2.3	Discovering a System and Installing an Agent
Overview	In this exercise, you will install the agent to the lab servers so that they can be managed by Operations Manager.
Mindset	You can use Operations Manager to monitor computers running Windows, UNIX, and Linux operating systems. To monitor a computer, the computer must be discovered and an agent must be installed; if not, you will have to install the agent manually.
Completion time	20 minutes

1. On Server02, in the Operations Manager console, click the **Administration** workspace.
2. In the left pane, under Device Management, click the **Agent Managed** node.
3. Right-click the **Agent Managed** node and choose **Discovery Wizard**.
4. In the Computer and Device Management Wizard, on the Discovery Type page, Windows computers is already selected. Click **Next**.
5. On the Auto or Advanced? page, the Advanced discovery option is already selected. Click **Next**.
6. On the Discovery Method page, select the **Browse for, or type-in computer names** option and then click **Browse**.
7. In the Select Computers dialog box, type the following and click **OK**:

   rwdc01

   server01

   server03

   vserver01

   vserver02

8. Back on the Discovery Method page, click **Next**.
9. On the Administrator Account page, Use selected Management Server Action Account is already selected. Answer the next question and click **Discover**.

Question 11	*What is the Management Server Action Account?*

10. On the Select Objects to Manage page, click the **Select All** button

Question 12	*What is the Management Server?*

Question 13	*What is the selected Management Mode?*

11. Click **Next**.

12. On the Summary page, answer the following question and click **Finish**.

Question 14	*What account will be used to run the agent?*

13. The Computer and Device Management Wizard closes and the Agent Management Task Status window opens. Expand the Agent Management Task Status dialog box so that you can see the status of the five servers.

14. When the agents for the five servers have been installed, close the Agent Management Task Status dialog box by clicking the **Close** button.

15. With the Agent Managed node selected, take a screen shot showing the five managed servers by pressing **Alt+Prt Scr** and then paste it into your Lab 2 worksheet file in the page provided by pressing **Ctrl+V**.

Leave the Operations Manager console open for the next exercise.

Exercise 2.4	Installing Management Packs
Overview	In this exercise, you will install multiple management packs, which will be needed for future exercises.
Mindset	When you want to monitor roles and features, you must install the management pack for the specific role or feature. For example, you can download and install the DHCP management pack so that you can monitor the DHCP role. In addition, you can download and install management packs for Microsoft products, such as Microsoft SQL Server and Microsoft Exchange.
Completion time	30 minutes

1. On Server02, in the Administration workspace, click **Management Packs** and review the list of management packs deployed to Operations Manager.

Question 15	*What version does the Windows Core Library have?*

Question 16	*What version does the Windows Server Operating System Library have?*

2. In the Tasks pane, click **Import Management Packs**.

3. In the Import Management Packs dialog box, click **Add**, and then, in the Add drop-down list box, click **Add from disk**.

4. In the Select Management Online Catalog Connection dialog box, click **Yes**. If a message indicates that the Operations Manager cannot connect to the Web service, click **Close**.

5. In the Select Management Packs to import dialog box, in the File name text box, type **\\rwdc01\software\ManagementPacks** and press **Enter**. Then highlight all of the management packs by clicking the first management pack and pressing the **Shift** key. With the Shift key pressed, use the down arrow key until all management packs are highlighted. Click **Open**.

6. Back on the Select Management Packs page, click **Install**. If you a message prompts you to confirm that you want to continue, click **Yes**.

7. It will take 20 to 25 minutes for all of the management packs to load. When the management packs are imported, click **Close**.

8. Take a screen shot showing the management packs by pressing **Alt+Prt Scr** and then paste it into your Lab 2 worksheet file in the page provided by pressing **Ctrl+V**.

End of exercise. Close Operations Manager console and any other Windows that you have opened.

Lab Challenge	Designing Operations Manager Deployment (Operations Manager Deployment Project)
Overview	You are new administrator for the Contoso Corporation, which produces smart devices for the home. Read Appendix A for background information about the company and then read the information presented in this exercise.
Mindset	Over the past three years, your company has grown from 25 servers to more than 100 servers. You need to monitor these servers more effectively. Therefore, you need to develop a plan to monitor these servers.
Completion time	60 minutes

Create a proposal that includes the following sections:

- Purpose of the Project
- Requirements of the Project
- The Proposed Solution

When writing the proposal, you must explain the reasoning behind your choices.

End of lab. You can log off or start a different lab. If you want to restart this lab, you'll need to click the End Lab button in order for the lab to be reset.

LAB 3 PLANNING AND IMPLEMENTING AUTOMATED REMEDIATION

THIS LAB CONTAINS THE FOLLOWING EXERCISES AND ACTIVITIES:

Exercise 3.1	Installing WSUS
Exercise 3.2	Installing SQL Server Report Server
Exercise 3.3	Installing Operations Manager Reports
Exercise 3.4	Creating a Desired Configuration Manager (DCM) Baseline
Lab Challenge	Designing an Update Solution Project

BEFORE YOU BEGIN

The lab environment consists of student workstations connected to a local area network, along with a server that functions as the domain controller for a domain called contoso.com. The computers required for this lab are listed in Table 3-1.

Table 3-1
Computers required for Lab 3

Computer	*Operating System*	*Computer Name*
Server	Windows Server 2012 R2	RWDC01
Server	Windows Server 2012 R2	Server01
Server	Windows Server 2012 R2	Server02
Server	Windows Server 2012 R2	Server03

In addition to the computers, you will also need the software listed in Table 3-2 to complete Lab 3.

Table 3-2
Software required for Lab 3

Software	*Location*
SQL Server 2012 with SP1 installation files	\\rwdc01\software
System Center 2012 R2 Operations Manager Installation files	\\rwdc01\software
Lab 3 student worksheet	Lab03_worksheet.docx (provided by instructor)

Working with Lab Worksheets

Each lab in this manual requires that you answer questions, shoot screen shots, and perform other activities that you will document in a worksheet named for the lab, such as Lab03_worksheet.docx. You will find these worksheets on the book companion site. It is recommended that you use a USB flash drive to store your worksheets, so you can submit them to your instructor for review. As you perform the exercises in each lab, open the appropriate worksheet file, fill in the required information, and then save the file to your flash drive.

SCENARIO

After completing this lab, you will be able to:

- Install WSUS
- Install SQL Server Report Server
- Install Operations Manager Reports
- Create a Desired Configuration Manager (DCM) Baseline

Estimated lab time: 180 minutes

Exercise 3.1	Installing WSUS
Overview	In this exercise, you will install WSUS on the same server on which you have installed Configuration Manager.
Mindset	WSUS is part of the update mechanism for System Center 2012 R2 Configuration Manager and Virtual Machine Manager (VMM). Configuration Manager integrates with WSUS to find and download the various updates for Microsoft products and then uses its own distribution infrastructure to schedule and install the updates. Configuration Manager enables you to integrate the installation of updates into new systems that are deployed so that the new operating system deployments contain the latest approved updates.
Completion time	25 minutes

1. On Server01, log on using the **contoso\administrator** account and the **Pa$$w0rd** password.
2. Using File Explorer, create a **C:\Updates** folder.
3. If Server Manager is not open, open **Server Manager**. At the top of Server Manager, click **Manage > Add Roles and Features**. The Add Roles and Feature Wizard displays.
4. On the Before you begin page, click **Next**.
5. Select Role-based or feature-based installation and then click **Next**.
6. On the Select destination server page, click **Next**.
7. Scroll down and select **Windows Server Update Services**.
8. In the Add Roles and Features Wizard, click **Add Features**.
9. Back on the Select server roles screen, click **Next**.
10. On the Select features page, click **Next**.
11. On the Windows Server Update Services page, click **Next**.
12. By default, WID Database and WSUS Services are selected. Click **Next**.
13. In the Content location selection text box, type **C:\Updates** and then click **Next**.

NOTE	*Remember, if this was a production environment, you would store the updates on a non-system drive.*

14. On the Confirm installation selections page, click **Install**.

15. When the installation has completed, take a screen shot of the Add Roles and Features Wizard by pressing **Alt+Prt Scr** and then paste it into your Lab 3 worksheet file in the page provided by pressing **Ctrl+V**.

16. Click **Close**.

17. Using Server Manager, click **Tools > Windows Server Update Services**.

18. In the Complete WSUS Installation dialog box, click **Run**.

19. When the post-installation is successfully completed, click **Close**.

20. On the Before You Begin page, click **Next**.

21. On the Join the Microsoft Update Improvement Program page, clear the **Yes, I would like to join the Microsoft Update Improvement Program** check box, then click **Next**.

22. When the Choose Upstream Server page displays, click **Synchronize from another Windows Server Update Services server**. In the Server name text box, type **RWDC01.contoso.com**. Answer the following question and then click **Next**.

Question 1	*After synchronizing from another WSUS server, what default port is used?*

23. On the Specify Proxy Server page, click **Next**.

24. On the Connect to Upstream Server page, click **Start Connecting**.

25. When the connection is complete, click **Next**.

26. On the Choose Languages page, click **Next**.

27. On the Set Sync Schedule page, click **Next**.

28. On the Finished page, select **Begin initial synchronization** and then click **Next**.

29. On the What's Next page, click **Finish**.

30. On the WSUS console, expand **Server01** and then click **Synchronizations**. It will take a couple minutes for the synchronization to occur, as shown under Synchronization Status in the bottom pane.

End of exercise. You can close the WSUS console on Server01.

Exercise 3.2	Installing SQL Server Report Server
Overview	In this exercise, you will install the SQL Server Report Server on the same server that Operations Manager is installed.
Mindset	Operations Manager uses SQL Server Report Server (SSRS) to create, manage, and store reports. SSRS allows for the creating and retrieval of reports.
Completion time	40 minutes

1. On Server02, log on using the **contoso\administrator** account and the **Pa$$w0rd** password.

2. On the task bar, click the **File Explorer** icon. Then open the **rwdc01\software** folder.

3. Double-click the SQL Server 2012 with SP1 ISO file.

4. Double-click the **setup** application.

5. When the SQL Server Installation Center opens, click **Installation**.

6. Click **New SQL Server stand-alone installation or add features to an existing installation**.

7. When the SQL Server 2012 Setup wizard opens, on the Setup Support Rules page, click **OK**.

8. On the Product Updates page, deselect the **Include SQL Server product updates** option and then click **Next**.

9. On the Setup Support Rules page, click **Next**.

10. On the Product Key page, click **Next**.

11. On the License Terms page, select **I accept the license terms** option and then click **Next**.

12. If the Product Updates page appears, click **Next**.

13. On the Setup Role page, click **Next**. If a message indicates that a computer restart is required, click **OK**. Reboot the computer and then restart the SQL installation.

14. On the Feature Selection page, select **Reporting Services – Native.**

Question 2	*What prerequisite still needs to be installed?*

15. Click **Next**.
16. On the Installation Rules page, click **Next**.
17. On the Instance Configuration page, click **Next**.
18. On the Disk Space Requirements page, click **Next**.
19. On the Server Configuration page, click **Next**.
20. On the Reporting Services Configuration page, click **Next**.
21. On the Error Reporting page, click **Next**.
22. On the Installation Configuration Rules page, click **Next**.
23. On the Ready to Install page, click **Install**.
24. Take a screen shot of the SQL Server 2012 Setup by pressing **Alt+Prt Scr** and then paste it into your Lab 3 worksheet file in the page provided by pressing **Ctrl+V**.
25. Click **Close.**
26. Click the **Start** button and then click the **Show All Programs** button (down arrow). Then under Microsoft SQL Server 2012, click **Reporting Services Configuration Manager**.
27. In Reporting Services Configuration Manager, the Reporting Services Configuration Connection dialog box opens. Click **Connect**.
28. Click **Web Service URL**.

Question 3	*What is the Report Server Web Service URLs?*

29. Click **Apply**.
30. Click **Database**.
31. Click **Change Database**.
32. In the Report Server Database Configuration Wizard, on the Action page, Create a new report server database is already selected. Click **Next**.
33. On the Database Server page, for the Server Name, type **Server03**. Click **Next**.
34. On the Database page, answer the following question and then click **Next**.

Question 4	*What is the Database Name?*

35. On the Credentials page, for the Authentication Type, select **Windows Credentials**. In the User name (Domain\user) text box, type **contoso\administrator**. For the Password text box, type **Pa$$w0rd**. Click **Next**.

36. On the Change Database page, click **Next**. The installation will start and may take a couple of minutes

37. On the Summary page, click **Next**.

38. When the database is created, take a screen shot of the Report Server Database Configuration wizard by pressing **Alt+Prt Scr** and then paste it into your Lab 3 worksheet file in the page provided by pressing **Ctrl+V**.

39. Click **Finish**.

40. Click **Report Manager URL**.

Question 5	*What is the URL for Report Manager?*

41. Click **Apply**.

42. Click **Exit**.

End of exercise. Close all windows.

Exercise 3.3	Installing Operations Manager Reports
Overview	In this exercise, you will install the Operations Manager Reports to the current Operations Management installation.
Mindset	To view the reports that are available in Operations Manager, you have to install the Reports component. Most reports allow you to aggregate data by day, week, or month.
Completion time	15 minutes

1. On Server02, on the task bar, click the **File Explorer** icon. Then open the **\\rwdc01\software** folder.

2. Using Server Manager, click **Tools** > **Services**.

3. Make sure the Remote Registry setting is running. If it is not, right-click the **Remote Registry** service and choose **Start**.

4. If you have the System Center 2012 R2 Operations Manager ISO file, double-click the **System Center 2012 R2 Operations Manager ISO** file. If you have a SC2012 R2 SCOSM folder, double-click the **SC2012 R2 SCOM** folder.

5. Double-click the **Setup** application.

6. In the Operations Manager window, click **Install.**

7. In the Operations Manager Setup window, click **Add a feature**.

8. On the Select features to install page, select **Reporting server** and then click **Next**.

9. On the Prerequisites page, click **Next**.

10. On the Configuration page, the SQL Server instance is Server02. Click **Next**.

11. On the Configure Operations Manager accounts page, for the Data Reader account Domain\User Name text box, type **contoso\administrator**. For the password, type **Pa$$w0rd**. Click **Next**.

12. On the Help improve Operations Manager, select the second **No, I am not willing to participate** option. Click **Next**.

13. On the Microsoft Update page, select **Off**. Then click **Next**.

14. On the Installation Summary page, click **Install**. The installation will take a few minutes.

15. When the Operations Manager Setup is installed successfully, take a screen shot of the Operations Manager Setup wizard by pressing **Alt+Prt Scr** and then paste it into your Lab 3 worksheet file in the page provided by pressing **Ctrl+V**.

Question 6	*What workspace allows you manage your reports in Operations Manager?*

End of exercise. Close all windows.

Exercise 3.4	Creating a Desired Configuration Manager (DCM) Baseline
Overview	In this exercise, you will create a Desired Configuration Manager Baseline (DCM) and deploy the DCM to a designated collection.
Mindset	Configuration Manager allows you to manage the configuration and compliance of servers, laptops, desktop computers, and mobile devices in your organization using DCM. With DCM, you can define a configuration baseline that contains the configuration items that you want to evaluate and settings and rules that describe the level of compliance. You then deploy DCM to users and devices through Configuration Manager collections and a defined schedule.
Completion time	40 minutes

1. On Server01, log on using the **contoso\administrator** account and the **Pa$$w0rd** password.

2. Click the **Start** button, click the **Show All Programs** button (down arrow), and under the Microsoft System Center 2012 R2 section, click **Configuration Manager Console**.

3. In the Configuration Manager console, click the **Administration** workspace.

4. Expand the **Site Configuration** node and then click the **Servers and Site System Roles**.

5. In the main pane, right-click **Server01** and choose **Add Site System Roles**.

6. In the Add Site System Roles Wizard, on the General page, click **Next**.

7. On the Specify Internet proxy server page, click **Next**.

8. On the System Role Selection page, move the mouse pointer to a red circle with a white exclamation point appears. A description of the error appears

Question 7	*What is the error that appears?*

9. On the System Role Selection page, click **Software update point** and then click **Next**.

10. On the Software Update Point page, select the **WSUS is configured to use ports 8530 and 8531 for client communications (default settings for WSUS on Windows Server 2012)** option. Click **Next**.

11. On the Proxy and Account Settings page, select the **Use credentials to connect to the WSUS server** option. Click the **Set** button and select **Existing Account**. In the Select Account dialog box, double-click **contoso\administrator**. Back on the Proxy and Account Settings page, click **Next**.

12. On the Synchronization Source page, select **Synchronize from an upstream data source location (URL)** option. Then in the text box, type the following and then click **Next**:

    http://server01.contoso.com:8530

13. On the Synchronization Schedule page, select the **Enable synchronization on a schedule** option.

Question 8	*By default, how often does Configuration Manager perform an update?*

14. Click **Next**.

15. On the Supersedence Rules page, click **Next**.

16. On the Classifications page, answer the following question. Then select **Critical Updates** and then click **Next**.

Question 9	*What classifications are already chosen?*

17. On the Products page, expand **All Products > Microsoft > Windows**. Select only **Windows Server 2012**, leaving the rest unselected.

18. **Navigate to All Products > Microsoft > Office**. Deselect all versions of Office. Click **Next**.

NOTE	*When you perform the first synchronization with Microsoft Update site, the product list will also be updated. Therefore, after the first synchronization, Windows Server 2012 R2 would appear.*

19. On the Languages page, make sure that English is the only language selected. Click **Next**.

20. On the Summary page, click **Next**.

21. When the site system role wizard has completed successfully, take a screen shot of the Add Site System Roles Wizard by pressing **Alt+Prt Scr** and then paste it into your Lab 3 worksheet file in the page provided by pressing **Ctrl+V**.

22. Click **Close**.

23. Click the **Software Library** workspace.

24. Expand the **Software Updates** node. Then right-click the **All Software Updates** node and choose **Synchronize Software Updates**. When you are prompted to run synchronization, click **Yes**.

25. WSUS will start a synchronization, which can be monitored from the WSUS console by clicking the **Monitoring** workspace. Then click the **Software Update Point Synchronization Status** node.

26. When the synchronization finishes, go back to the **Software Library** workspace and then click **Software Updates\All Software Updates**.

27. In the ribbon, click **Synchronize Software Updates**. Click **Yes** to initiate a site-wide synchronization of software updates.

28. On the ribbon click the **Run Summarization** button. In the Configuration manager dialog box, click **OK**.

29. After a couple of minutes, go back to the **Administration** workspace. Under the Site Configuration node, click the **Sites** node.

30. Right-click the **001 – Corporate** site and choose **Configure Site Components > Software Update Point**.

31. In the Software Update Point Component Properties dialog box, click the **Products** tab.

32. Deselect **Windows Server 2012** and select **Windows Server 2012 R2**.

33. Click **OK** to close the Software Update Point Component Properties dialog box.

34. Go back to the **Software Library** workspace. Click **Synchronize Software Updates**. When you are prompted to run synchronization, click **Yes**. Wait about 5 minutes and then press the **F5** key to refresh.

35. Click the **Assets and Compliance** workspace.

36. Under Overview, click **User Collections**. Then right-click **User Collections** and choose **Create User Collection**.

37. In the Create User Collection Wizard, on the General Page, in the Name text box, type **Clients Needing Updates**.

38. Click the Browse button. In the Select Collection dialog box, double-click **All Users and User Groups**. Back on the General page, click **Next**.

39. On the Membership Rules page, click **Next**. When a warning states that this collection has no member rules, click **OK**.

40. On the Summary page, click **Next**.

41. On the Completion page, click **Close**.

42. Expand the **Compliance Settings** node and then click the **Configuration Baselines** node.

43. In the ribbon, click **Create Configuration Baseline**.

44. In the Create Configuration Baseline dialog box, in the Name text box, type **ConfigurationBaseline01**.

45. Click the **Add** button and then click **Software Updates**.

46. Under Classifications, expand **Security Updates > Microsoft** and then click **Windows Server 2012 R2**. Select the first five updates and then click **OK**.

47. Close the Create Configuration Baseline dialog box by clicking **OK**.

48. To deploy a configuration baseline, on the ribbon, click **Deploy**.

49. To remediate the systems, select **Remediate noncompliant rules when supported**.

50. Click the **Browse** button. In the Select Collection dialog box, double-click **Clients Needing Updates**.

51. Under the Schedule section, the configuration baseline is configured to be deployed every 7 days. Click **OK**.

52. At the bottom of the screen, click the **Deployments** tab.

53. Take a screen shot of the configuration baseline by pressing **Alt+Prt Scr** and then paste it into your Lab 3 worksheet file in the page provided by pressing **Ctrl+V**.

End of exercise. Close all Windows and programs.

Lab Challenge	Designing an Update Solution Project
Overview	You are an administrator for the Contoso Corporation, which produces smart devices for the home. Read Appendix A for background information about the company and then read the information presented in this exercise.
Mindset	Because you now have a lot more servers to manage, you need to come up with a more efficient way to keep these systems updated. Therefore, you need to develop a plan that updates your systems and keeps them updated.
Completion time	60 minutes

Create a proposal that includes the following sections:

- Purpose of the Project
- Requirements of the Project
- The Proposed Solution

When writing the proposal, you must explain the reasoning behind your choices.

End of lab. You can log off or start a different lab. If you want to restart this lab, you'll need to click the End Lab button in order for the lab to be reset.

LAB 4
PLANNING AND IMPLEMENTING FAILOVER CLUSTER

THIS LAB CONTAINS THE FOLLOWING EXERCISES AND ACTIVITIES:

Exercise 4.1	Planning a Failover Solution
Exercise 4.2	Implementing Central Storage for Clustering
Exercise 4.3	Implementing a Failover Cluster
Lab Challenge	Designing a Failover Solution Project I

BEFORE YOU BEGIN

The lab environment consists of student workstations connected to a local area network, along with a server that functions as the domain controller for a domain called contoso.com. The computers required for this lab are listed in Table 4-1.

Table 4-1
Computers required for Lab 4

Computer	***Operating System***	***Computer Name***
Server	Windows Server 2012 R2	RWDC01
Server	Windows Server 2012 R2	VServer01
Server	Windows Server 2012 R2	VServer02
Server	Windows Server 2012 R2	Server03

In addition to the computers, you will also need the software listed in Table 4-2 to complete Lab 4.

Table 4-2
Software required for Lab 4

Software	***Location***
Lab 4 student worksheet	Lab04_worksheet.docx (provided by instructor)

Working with Lab Worksheets

Each lab in this manual requires that you answer questions, shoot screen shots, and perform other activities that you will document in a worksheet named for the lab, such as Lab04_worksheet.docx. You will find these worksheets on the book companion site. It is recommended that you use a USB flash drive to store your worksheets, so you can submit them to your instructor for review. As you perform the exercises in each lab, open the appropriate worksheet file, fill in the required information, and then save the file to your flash drive.

SCENARIO

After completing this lab, you will be able to:

- Plan and design a failover cluster
- Implement central storage for a failover cluster
- Implement a failover cluster

Estimated lab time: 200 minutes

Exercise 4.1	Planning a Failover Solution
Overview	In this written exercise, you will read the background information for the Contoso Corporation found in Appendix A. You will then read the information introduced in this lesson and answer the questions.
Mindset	Over the past year, you had several failures that greatly affected the corporation. So while you know that you will not be able to stop every failure, you want to reduce the number of failures and you want to reduce the effects of those failures. Therefore, you decide to use failover clusters for your critical services.
Completion time	20 minutes

Question 1	*Which servers within the organization would you recommend to use on a failover cluster?*

Question 2	*If you decide to use a failover cluster for a database server how many servers would you use and what type of quorum would you use? Explain your answer.*

Question 3	*What storage requirements would you need with this failover cluster?*

Question 4	*You decide to make an important file server into a failover cluster. Which type of failover cluster (General Use File Server or Scale-Out File Server) should be used if you want to also support DFS?*

Question 5	*Which type of disks do you need to use with a Scale-Out File Server?*

Question 6	*After you set these clusters, you now want to keep these servers updated with the newest Microsoft Windows updates. What can you use to update the servers automatically without any down time?*

Exercise 4.2	Implementing Central Storage for Clustering
Overview	In this exercise, you will create an iSCSI target on Server03, which will be used by VServer01 and VServer02. Unlike previous courses, you will not be guided through each step. Instead, you must determine the best way to deploy the application based on the guidelines provided.
Mindset	Because clusters usually need to access shared storage, the cluster should have a public-and-private network to communicate with the shared storage. If the cluster communicates to shared storage using Fibre Channel, the Fibre Channel will connect using a dedicated network known as a fabric.
Completion time	60 minutes

On Server03, create the following iSCSI target disks:

- ShareDisk (5 GB)
- QuorumDisk (2 GB)

Take a screenshot of the iSCSI page showing the two iSCSI Virtual Disks.

Then on VServer01 and VServer02, use the iSCSI Initiator to add the disks to the systems. On VServer01, use Computer Management to prepare and format the disks. Lastly, take a screenshot of Computer Management of the prepared disks.

Exercise 4.3	Implementing a Failover Cluster
Overview	In this exercise, you will create a failover cluster with VServer01 and VServer02. Unlike the approach used in previous courses, you will not be guided through each step. Instead, you must determine the best way to deploy the application based on the guidelines provided.
Mindset	A failover cluster is a set of servers that work together to increase the availability of services and applications. The clustered servers (also known as nodes) are connected through a network connection (physical or virtual) and by software. If one a node fails, another node begins to provide services (a process known as failover).
Completion time	60 minutes

On VServer01 and VServer02, create a failover cluster called Cluster01 assigned to the IP address of 192.168.1.120. Take a screenshot of the cluster successfully validated showing the Overall Result and take a screenshot of Cluster Manager showing the new cluster. Hint: Check the IP configuration of both network adapters on Vserver01 and VServer02.

Lab Challenge	Designing a Failover Solution Project I
Overview	You are an administrator for the Contoso Corporation, which produces smart devices for the home. Read Appendix A for background information about the company and then read the information presented in this exercise.
Mindset	Because your company has grown, it is not more important that you minimize downtime. Therefore, you need to create a plan that identifies the servers that you will convert to a failover cluster and then make a plan to convert those servers into a cluster.
Completion time	60 minutes

Create a proposal that includes the following sections:

- Purpose of the Project
- Requirements of the Project
- The Proposed Solution

When writing the proposal, you must explain the reasoning behind your choices.

End of lab. You can log off or start a different lab. If you want to restart this lab, you'll need to click the End Lab button in order for the lab to be reset.

LAB 5
PLANNING AND IMPLEMENTING HIGHLY AVAILABLE NETWORK SERVICES

THIS LAB CONTAINS THE FOLLOWING EXERCISES AND ACTIVITIES:

Exercise 5.1	Planning a Highly Available Network Services
Exercise 5.2	Implementing a NLB Cluster
Lab Challenge	Designing a NLB Deployment

BEFORE YOU BEGIN

The lab environment consists of student workstations connected to a local area network, along with a server that functions as the domain controller for a domain called contoso.com. The computers required for this lab are listed in Table 5-1.

Table 5-1
Computers required for Lab 5

Computer	*Operating System*	*Computer Name*
Server	Windows Server 2012 R2	RWDC01
Server	Windows Server 2012 R2	Server01
Server	Windows Server 2012 R2	Server02
Server	Windows Server 2012 R2	Server03

In addition to the computers, you will also need the software listed in Table 5-2 to complete Lab 5.

Table 5-2
Software required for Lab 5

Software	*Location*
Lab 5 student worksheet	Lab05_worksheet.docx (provided by instructor)

Working with Lab Worksheets

Each lab in this manual requires that you answer questions, shoot screen shots, and perform other activities that you will document in a worksheet named for the lab, such as Lab05_worksheet.docx. You will find these worksheets on the book companion site. It is recommended that you use a USB flash drive to store your worksheets, so you can submit them to your instructor for review. As you perform the exercises in each lab, open the appropriate worksheet file, fill in the required information, and then save the file to your flash drive.

SCENARIO

After completing this lab, you will be able to:

- Plan and design a highly available network services using an NLB cluster
- Implement a NLB cluster

Estimated lab time: 120 minutes

Exercise 5.1	Planning a Highly Available Network Services
Overview	In this written exercise, you will read the background information for the Contoso Corporation found in Appendix A. You will then read the information introduced in this lesson and answer the questions.
Mindset	Over the past year, you have a several failures that greatly affected the corporation. You are considering using failover clusters, but you also need to consider Network Load Balancing (NLB), which can be used reduce the number of server failures as well as the effects of those failures.
Completion time	15 minutes

Question 1	*When creating a NLB cluster, what is the minimum and maximum number of nodes per cluster can you use?*

Question 2	*For the Contoso Corporation, which servers should be part of an NLB cluster?*

Question 3	*If these are normal internal and external web servers, which ports should you configure the port rules for?*

Question 4	*If you want maximum scalability, which filter mode would you use?*

Question 5	*If you decide to use unicast mode, how many network adapters should you have for each node?*

Question 6	*If you decide to use multicast mode, how many network adapters should you have for each node?*

Exercise 5.2	Implementing a NLB Cluster
Overview	In this exercise, you will create a Network Load Balancing (NLB) cluster with Server01 and Server02. Unlike the approach used in previous courses, you will not be guided through each step. Instead, you must determine the best way to deploy the application based on the guidelines provided.
Mindset	NLB transparently distributes traffic across multiple servers by using virtual IP addresses and a shared name. With NLB, you gain fault tolerance and enhanced performance. It is often used with mission-critical web servers but can also be found with other types of servers.
Completion time	45 minutes

On Server01 and Server02, create a Network Load Balancing cluster that will provide highly available web servers using the IP address of 192.168.1.130. Take a screenshot of the cluster in the Network Load Balancing Manager console.

Lab Challenge	Designing an NLB Deployment
Overview	You are an administrator for the Contoso Corporation, which produces smart devices for the home. Read Appendix A for background information about the company and then read the information presented in this exercise.
Mindset	Because your company has grown, it has become more important to minimize downtime. Therefore, you need to create a plan that identifies the servers that you will convert to a Network Load Balancing cluster and then make a plan to convert those servers into a cluster.
Completion time	60 minutes

Create a proposal that includes the following sections:

- Purpose of the Project
- Requirements of the Project
- The Proposed Solution

When writing the proposal, you must explain the reasoning behind your choices.

End of lab. You can log off or start a different lab. If you want to restart this lab, you'll need to click the End Lab button in order for the lab to be reset.

LAB 6
PLANNING AND IMPLEMENTING HIGHLY AVAILABLE STORAGE SOLUTIONS

THIS LAB CONTAINS THE FOLLOWING EXERCISES AND ACTIVITIES:

Exercise 6.1	Planning a Highly Available Storage Solution
Exercise 6.2	Creating a Clustered Storage Space
Lab Challenge	Designing a Highly Available Storage Solution Project

BEFORE YOU BEGIN

The lab environment consists of student workstations connected to a local area network, along with a server that functions as the domain controller for a domain called contoso.com. The computers required for this lab are listed in Table 6-1.

Table 6-1
Computers required for Lab 6

Computer	*Operating System*	*Computer Name*
Server	Windows Server 2012 R2	RWDC01
Server	Windows Server 2012 R2	VServer01
Server	Windows Server 2012 R2	VServer02
Server	Windows Server 2012 R2	Server03

In addition to the computers, you will also need the software listed in Table 6-2 to complete Lab 6.

Table 6-2
Software required for Lab 6

Software	*Location*
Lab 6 student worksheet	Lab06_worksheet.docx (provided by instructor)

Working with Lab Worksheets

Each lab in this manual requires that you answer questions, shoot screen shots, and perform other activities that you will document in a worksheet named for the lab, such as Lab06_worksheet.docx. You will find these worksheets on the book companion site. It is recommended that you use a USB flash drive to store your worksheets, so you can submit them to your instructor for review. As you perform the exercises in each lab, open the appropriate worksheet file, fill in the required information, and then save the file to your flash drive.

SCENARIO

After completing this lab, you will be able to:

- Plan and design a highly available storage solution
- Create a clustered storage space

Estimated lab time: 130 minutes

Exercise 6.1	Planning a Highly Available Storage Solution
Overview	In this written exercise, you will read the background information for the Contoso Corporation found in Appendix A. You will then read the information introduced in this lesson and answer the questions.
Mindset	Since the number of servers has increased dramatically over the past couple of years, you need to plan for and design highly available storage solutions.
Completion time	20 minutes

Question 1	*Which two technologies are used to provide resilient, highly available, cost-efficient storage solution?*

Question 2	*If you want to have a two-way mirror storage space, how many drives do you need?*

Question 3	*In a storage space, how many drives do you need in order to protect against two simultaneous drive failures?*

Question 4	*How do you make domain-based DFS namespace highly available?*

Question 5	*How do you make a stand-alone DFS namespace highly available?*

Question 6	*When using DFS namespace, which referrals should be used when you want users to use a particular DFS server first and, when that server is unavailable, then use other servers?*

Question 7	*You have a shared folder that you must make highly available. What can you do?*

Question 8	*Your SAN is based on iSCSI. You need to ensure that your servers have highly available connections to the SAN. What should you do?*

Question 9	*What kind of network connections should be used to connect the SAN to the blades in the chassis?*

Exercise 6.2	Creating a Clustered Storage Space
Overview	In this exercise, you will create three iSCSI virtual disks (Disk1, Disk2, and Disk3) on Server03. You will then use those disks to create a clustered storage space.
Mindset	A clustered storage space combines storage spaces and a failover cluster to provide a resilient, highly available, and cost-efficient storage solution. To provide resilience and redundancy, you connect to a just-a-bunch-of disk enclosures from multiple servers. To create a clustered storage space, you must have at least three physical disks, with at least 4 gigabytes (GB) each. These disks can be connected through iSCSI.
Completion time	50 minutes

1. On Server03, log on using the **contoso\administrator** account and the **Pa$$w0rd** password.
2. In Server Manager, click **File and Storage Services** and then click **iSCSI**.
3. Click **Tasks** > **New iSCSI Virtual Disk**.
4. When the New iSCSI Virtual Disk Wizard starts, click **Next**.
5. On the Specify iSCSI virtual disk name page, type **Disk1** and then click **Next**.
6. Specify **5 GB** and then click **Next**.
7. On the Assign iSCSI target page, Existing iSCSI target is already selected. Click **ClusterServers** and then click **Next**.
8. On the Confirm selections page, click **Create**.
9. When the iSCSI virtual disk is created, click **Close**.
10. Click **Tasks** > **New iSCSI Virtual Disk**.
11. When the New iSCSI Virtual Disk Wizard starts, click **Next**.
12. On the Specify iSCSI virtual disk name page, type **Disk2** and then click **Next**.

13. Specify **5 GB** and then click **Next**.
14. On the Assign iSCSI target page, Existing iSCSI target is already selected. Click **ClusterServers** and then click **Next**.
15. On the Confirm selections page, click **Create**.
16. When the iSCSI virtual disk is created, click **Close**.
17. Click **Tasks** > **New iSCSI Virtual Disk**.
18. When the New iSCSI Virtual Disk Wizard starts, click **Next**.
19. On the Specify iSCSI virtual disk name page, type **Disk3** and then click **Next**.
20. Specify **5 GB** and then click **Next**.
21. On the Assign iSCSI target page, Existing iSCSI target is already selected. Click **ClusterServers** and then click **Next**.
22. On the Confirm selections page, click **Create**.
23. When the iSCSI virtual disk is created, click **Close**.
24. If any of the disks are not connected, press the **F5** key.
25. Take a screen shot of the Server Manager console by pressing **Alt+Prt Scr** and then paste it into your Lab 6 worksheet file in the page provided by pressing **Ctrl+V**.
26. On VServer01, log on using the **contoso\administrator** account and the **Pa$$w0rd** password. Reboot VServer01.
27. On VServer02, log on using the **contoso\administrator** account and the **Pa$$w0rd** password. Reboot VServer02.
28. On VServer01, log on using the **contoso\administrator** account and the **Pa$$w0rd** password.
29. Using Server Manager, click **Tools** > **iSCSI Initiator**.
30. Click the **Volumes and Devices** tab and then click **Auto Configure**.
31. To close the iSCSI Initiator Properties dialog box, click **OK**.
32. On VServer02, log on using the **contoso\administrator** account and the **Pa$$w0rd** password.
33. Using Server Manager, click **Tools** > **iSCSI Initiator**.
34. Click the **Volumes and Devices** tab and then click **Auto Configure**.

35. To close the iSCSI Initiator Properties dialog box, click **OK**.

36. On VServer01, using Server Manager, open **Failover Cluster Manager**.

37. Expand the **Cluster01.contoso.com** cluster and then expand the **Storage** node.

38. Right-click **Pools** and choose **New Storage Pool**.

39. In the New Storage Pool Wizard, on the Before you begin page, click **Next**.

40. On the Specify a Storage Pool name and subsystem page, in the Name text box, type **Pool1** and then click **Next**.

41. On the Select physical disks for the Storage Pool page, select the check box next to physical disk 3, 4 and 5. Click **Next**.

42. On the Confirm selections page, verify that the settings are correct and then click **Create**.

43. On the View results page, verify that all tasks are completed and then click **Close**. Under Storage, select the **Pools** node .

44. Take a screen shot of the Failover Cluster Manager console by pressing **Alt+Prt Scr** and then paste it into your Lab 6 worksheet file in the page provided by pressing **Ctrl+V**.

45. Right-click the **Cluster Pool 1** and choose **New Virtual Disk**.

46. In the New Virtual Disk Wizard, on the Before You Begin page, click **Next**.

47. On the Select the storage pool, select **Pool1** and then click **Next**.

48. On the Specify the virtual disk name, in the Name text box, type **VDisk1** and then click **Next**.

49. On the Select the storage layout page, click **Mirror** and then click **Next**.

50. In the Specify the size of the virtual disk page, for the disk size, specify **4 GB** and then click **Next**.

51. On the Confirm selections page, click **Create**.

52. On the View results page, verify that all tasks completed, make sure that the **Create a volume when this wizard closes** check box is selected, and then click **Close**.

53. In the New Volume Wizard, on the Before you begin page, click **Next**.

54. On the Select the server and disk page, in the Server area, click **Cluster01**.

55. In the Disk area, click the virtual disk that you just created. Click **Next**.

56. On the Specify the size of the volume page, specify **4 GB**. Click **Next**.

57. On the Assign to a drive letter or folder page, select the **G** drive. click **Next**.

58. On the Select file system settings page, in the File system list, in the Volume label text box, type **StorageSpace**.

Question 10	*What is the default file system?*

59. Click **Next**.

60. On the Confirm selections page, verify that the settings are correct and then click **Create**.

61. When the volume is created, take a screen shot of the New Volume Wizard by pressing **Alt+Prt Scr** and then paste it into your Lab 6 worksheet file in the page provided by pressing **Ctrl+V**.

62. Click **Close**.

Lab Challenge	Designing a Highly Available Storage Solution Project
Overview	You are an administrator for the Contoso Corporation, which produces smart devices for the home. Read Appendix A for background information about the company and then read the information presented in this exercise.
Mindset	At a manufacturing site, you have to create a fault-tolerant system that controls the manufacturing equipment. The server running Windows Server 2012 R2 at the manufacturing site contains 6 hard drives. In addition, inventory files are kept on a shared folder, which must be accessed by other corporate applications. Therefore, the shared folder must be fault-tolerant. Develop a plan to implement this system.
Completion time	60 minutes

Create a proposal that includes the following sections:

- Purpose of the Project
- Requirements of the Project
- The Proposed Solution

When writing the proposal, you must explain the reasoning behind your choices.

End of lab. You can log off or start a different lab. If you want to restart this lab, you'll need to click the End Lab button in order for the lab to be reset.

LAB 7
PLANNING AND IMPLEMENTING HIGHLY AVAILABLE ROLES

THIS LAB CONTAINS THE FOLLOWING EXERCISES AND ACTIVITIES:

Exercise 7.1	Planning Highly Available Roles
Exercise 7.2	Implementing Highly Available Hyper-V Clustering
Exercise 7.3	implementing the General Use File Server Role
Exercise 7.4	Deploying a Scale-Out File Server
Lab Challenge	Designing a Failover Solution Project II

BEFORE YOU BEGIN

The lab environment consists of student workstations connected to a local area network, along with a server that functions as the domain controller for a domain called contoso.com. The computers required for this lab are listed in Table 7-1.

Table 7-1
Computers required for Lab 7

Computer	*Operating System*	*Computer Name*
Server	Windows Server 2012 R2	RWDC01
Server	Windows Server 2012 R2	VServer01
Server	Windows Server 2012 R2	VServer02
Server	Windows Server 2012 R2	Server03

In addition to the computers, you will also need the software listed in Table 7-2 to complete Lab 7.

Table 7-2
Software required for Lab 7

Software	*Location*
Lab 7 student worksheet	Lab07_worksheet.docx (provided by instructor)

Working with Lab Worksheets

Each lab in this manual requires that you answer questions, shoot screen shots, and perform other activities that you will document in a worksheet named for the lab, such as Lab07_worksheet.docx. You will find these worksheets on the book companion site. It is recommended that you use a USB flash drive to store your worksheets, so you can submit them to your instructor for review. As you perform the exercises in each lab, open the appropriate worksheet file, fill in the required information, and then save the file to your flash drive.

SCENARIO

After completing this lab, you will be able to:

- Plan and design highly available roles
- Implement a highly available Hyper-V cluster
- Deploy a General Use File Server
- Deploy a Scale-Out File Server

Estimated lab time: 140 minutes

Exercise 7.1	Planning Highly Available Roles
Overview	In this written exercise, you will read the background information for the Contoso Corporation found in Appendix A. You will then read the information introduced in this lesson and answer the questions.
Mindset	Over the past year, you had several failures that greatly affected the corporation. So while you know that you will not be able to stop every failure, you want to reduce the number of failures and the effect of those failure. Therefore, you decide to use failover clusters for your critical services.
Completion time	20 minutes

Question 1	*When creating highly available roles, which type of clustered roles are DFS Namespace Server, DHCP Server, File Server, and Hyper-V Replica Broker?*

Question 2	*You need to make a highly available DHCP server. What three options do you have?*

Question 3	*If you decide to use a DHCP split-scope, what ratio should you use to specify the addresses assigned by the local DHCP server and the addresses assigned by the remote DHCP server?*

Question 4	*Of three highly available options for DHCP, which one allows addresses to be replicated to a central DHCP server?*

Question 5	*If you decide to use the DHCP failover, which mode specifies that one server handles the DHCP requests and the other server is idle?*

Question 6	*What is needed to use a DHCP split-scope or a DHCP failover so that DHCP requests are sent to a central located DHCP server?*

Question 7	*What is the location of the ShareDisk?*

Question 8	*If you need to use NFS or Data deduplication with a clustered file server, which type of clustered file server should you use?*

Question 9	*You have a third-party stateful application that you want to use on a failover cluster. Which type of role should you chose?*

Question 10	*You have a third-party stateless application that you want to use on a failover cluster. Which type of role should you chose?*

Exercise 7.2	Implementing Highly Available Hyper-V Clustering
Overview	In this exercise, you will implement a virtual machine on a failover cluster.
Mindset	It's common to use failover clusters with Hyper-V to provide highly available virtual machines (VMs). Of course, unlike other types of clusters, the Hyper-V nodes must be composed of physical hosts. You cannot run Hyper-V on a VM. In addition, to avoid losing network connectivity, you must create the same virtual networks on all physical hosts that participate in the cluster.
Completion time	30 minutes

1. On VServer01, log on using the **contoso\administrator** account and the **Pa$$w0rd** password.

2. Using Server Manager, click **Tools** > **Failover Cluster Manager**.

3. In the Failover Cluster Manager console, expand the **Cluster01.contoso.com** cluster, expand **Storage**, and click **Disks**.

4. Right-click **Cluster Disk 2** and choose **Add to Cluster Shared Volumes**.

Question 11	*What is the location of the ShareDisk?*

5. Using Server Manager, click **Tools** > **Hyper-V Manager**.

6. In the Hyper-V Manager, click **VSERVER01**. Then right-click **VSERVER01** and choose **New** > **Virtual Machine**.

7. In the New Virtual Machine Wizard, on the Before You Begin page, click **Next**.

8. On the Specify Name and Location page, in the Name text box, type **VM1**.

Question 12	*Where will the virtual machine be stored?*

9. Click the **Store the virtual machine in a different location** option and then click **Browse**.

10. In the Select Folder dialog box, navigate to the **C:\ClusterStorage\Volume1** folder. Click **Select Folder** and then click **Next**.

11. On the Specify Generation page, click **Next.**

12. On the Assign Memory page, in the Startup Memory text box, type **32**. Then click **Next**.

13. On the Configure Networking, click **Next**.

14. On the Connect Virtual Hard Disk page, for the size, specify **5** GB. Click **Next**.

15. On the Installation Options page, select **Next**.

16. On the Summary page, click **Finish**.

17. Go back to the Failover Cluster Manager console, right-click the **Roles** node and choose **Configure Role**.

18. In the High Availability Wizard, on the Before You Begin page, click **Next**.

19. On the Select Role page, click **Virtual Machine** and then click **Next**.

20. On the Select Virtual Machine page, select **VM1** and then click **Next**.

21. On the Confirmation page, click **Next**.

22. When the high availability is successful, take a screen shot of the High Availability Wizard by pressing **Alt+Prt Scr** and then paste it into your Lab 7 worksheet file in the page provided by pressing **Ctrl+V**.

23. Click **Finish**.

24. Right-click the **Roles** node and choose **Virtual Machines** > **New Virtual Machine**.

25. In the New Virtual Machine dialog box, double-click **VServer01**.

26. In the New Virtual Machine Wizard, on the Before You Begin page, click **Next**.

27. On the Specify Name and Location page, in the Name text box, type **VM2**. Answer the following question and then click **Next**.

Question 13	*Where is the virtual machine going to be stored?*

28. On the Specify Generation page, click **Next.**

29. On the Assign Memory page, in the Startup Memory text box, type **32**. Then click **Next**.

30. On the Configure Networking, click **Next**.

31. On the Connect Virtual Hard Disk page, for the size, specify **5** GB, click **Next**.

32. On the Installation Options page, select **Next**.

33. On the Summary page, click **Finish**.

34. On the second Summary page, click **Finish**.

35. After highlighting the Roles node, take a screen shot of the Failover Cluster Manager by pressing **Alt+Prt Scr** and then paste it into your Lab 7 worksheet file in the page provided by pressing **Ctrl+V**.

End of exercise. Close Hyper-V Manager but keep Failover Manager open for future exercises.

Exercise 7.3	Implementing the General Use File Server Role
Overview	To demonstrate using a failover cluster, you will create a General Use File Server using a failover cluster and the shared iSCSI drive.
Mindset	File servers in a cluster can be configured for general use using General Use File Server, which provides a central location for users to share files or for server applications that open and close files frequently. It also supports SMB, Network File System (NFS), Data Deduplication, File Server Resource Manager, DFS Replication, and other File Server role services.
Completion time	30 minutes

1. On VServer01, using Server Manager, click **Manage** > **Add Roles and Features**.
2. In the Add Roles and Features Wizard, On the Before you begin page, click **Next**.
3. On the Select installation type page, click **Next**.
4. On the Select destination server page, click **VServer01.contoso.com** and then click **Next**.
5. On the Select server roles page, expand **File and Storage Services**, expand **File and iSCSI Services**, and then select **File Server**. Click **Next**.
6. On the Features page, click **Next**.
7. On the Confirmation page, click **Install**. Once it is installed, click **Close**.
8. On VServer02, using Server Manager, click **Manage** > **Add Roles and Features**.
9. In the Add Roles and Features Wizard, On the Before you begin page, click **Next**.
10. On the Select installation type page, click **Next**.
11. On the Select destination server page, click **VServer02.contoso.com** and then click **Next**.
12. On the Select server roles page, expand File and Storage Services, expand **File and iSCSI Services**, and then select **File Server**. Click **Next**.
13. On the Features page, click **Next**.
14. On the Confirmation page, click **Install**. Once it is installed, click **Close**.
15. On VServer01, using the Failover Cluster Manager, right-click **Roles** and choose **Configure Role**.
16. In the High Availability Wizard, on the Before You Begin page, click **Next**.
17. On the Select Role page, click **File Server** and then click **Next**.
18. On the File Server Type page, click **File Server for general use** and then click **Next**.
19. On the Client Access Point page, in the Name text box, type **FileServer**. Type **192.168.1.140** in the Address column and then click **Next**.
20. On the Select Storage page, click to select the **Cluster Virtual Disk (VDisk1)** and then click **Next**.
21. On the Confirmation page, click **Next**.
22. On the Summary page, click **Finish**.
23. In the Failover Cluster Manager, click **Roles** (if it is not already selected or highlighted).

24. Take a screen shot of the Failover Cluster Manager by pressing **Alt+Prt Scr** and then paste it into your Lab 7 worksheet file in the page provided by pressing **Ctrl+V**.

25. Click **Cluster1.contoso.com**. If the Current Host Server is VServer01, right-click **Cluster1.contoso.com** and choose **More Actions** > **Move Core Cluster Resources** > **Select Node**. In the Move Cluster Resources dialog box, click **VServer02** and then click **OK**.

26. Click the **Roles** node. If the Owner node is VServer02, right-click File Server and choose **Move** > **Select Node**. In the Move Clustered Role dialog box, click **VServer01** and then click **OK**.

27. Wait two minutes to allow time for the DNS entry to be created for FileServer.

28. To create a file share, right-click the **File Server** role and choose **Add File Share**. If an error message displays, indicating the Client Access Point is not ready to be used for share creation, the DNS entry for FileServer has not been created. Click **OK**, wait a couple of minutes, and then try again.

29. In the New Share Wizard, click **SMB Share-Quick** and then click **Next**.

30. On the Share Location page, ensure the File Server cluster role is selected. Then with the **Type a custom path** selected, type **g:\data** in the text box. Click **Next**.

Question 14	*Which volume is available as a share location?*

31. On the Share Name page, in the Share name text box, type **Data1**.

Question 15	*What is the Local path to Share?*

Question 16	*What is the remote path to share?*

32. Click **Next**. When a message indicates the local path you entered does not exist, click **OK**.

33. On the Other settings page, select **Enable access-based enumeration** and then click **Next**.

34. On the Permissions page, view the current permissions and then click **Next**.

35. On the Confirmation page, click **Create**.

36. When the installation is complete, click **Close**.

37. With the FileServer role selected, click the **Resources** tab at the bottom of the console. You may need to resize the Failover Cluster Manager Windows to see the bottom tabs.

38. Take a screen shot of the Failover Cluster Manager by pressing **Alt+Prt Scr** and then paste it into your Lab 7 worksheet file in the page provided by pressing **Ctrl+V**.

39. Click the **Shares** tab.

40. Take a screen shot of the Failover Cluster Manager by pressing **Alt+Prt Scr** and then paste it into your Lab 7 worksheet file in the page provided by pressing **Ctrl+V**.

End of exercise. Leave the Failover Cluster Manager open for the next exercise.

Exercise 7.4	Deploying a Scale-Out File Server
Overview	In this exercise, you will remove the General Use File Server and install a Scale-Out File Server.
Mindset	Different from a General Use File Server cluster, the Scale-Out File Server cluster is an active-active failover cluster where all files shares are online on all nodes simultaneously. Although the Scale-Out File Server supports SMB, it does not support NFS, Data Deduplication, DFS Replication, or File Server Resource Manager. To support multiple nodes to access the same volume at the same time, the Scale-Out File Server uses a CSV.
Completion time	20 minutes

1. On VServer01, using Failover Cluster Manager, right-click the **FileServer** role and choose **Remove**. When you are prompted to confirm this action, click **Yes**.

2. On VServer01, right-click **Roles** and choose **Configure Role**.

3. In the High Availability Wizard, click **Next**.

4. On the Select Role page, click **File Server** and then click **Next**.

5. On the File Server Type page, click **Scale-Out File Server for application data** and then click **Next**.

6. On the Client Access Point page, type **FileServer2** in the Name text box. Click **Next**.

7. On the Confirmation page, click **Next**.

8. On the Summary page, click **Finish**.

9. Wait two minutes so that DNS entries have time to be created.

10. Click the **Roles** node. If the Owner node is VServer02, right-click **File Server** and choose **Move** > **Select Node**. In the Move Clustered Role dialog box, click V**Server01** and then click **OK**.

11. Click **Roles**. Right-click the **FileServer2** role and choose **Add File Share**. Click **OK**.

    If an error message displays, indicating the Client Access Point is not ready to be used for share creation, the DNS entry for FileServer has not been created. Wait a couple of minutes, and then try again.

12. In the New Share Wizard, click **SMB Share – Quick** and then click **Next**.

13. On the Share Location page, click the **FileServer2.**

Question 17	*What is the share location?*

14. Click **Next**.

15. On the Share Name page, type **Data2** in the Share name text box.

Question 18	*What is the remote path to share?*

16. Click **Next**.

17. On the Other Settings page, click to select **Enable access-based enumeration** and then click **Next**.

18. On the Permissions page, click **Next**.

19. On the Confirm selections page, click **Create**.

20. When the installation is complete, click **Close**.

21. With the **FileServer2** highlighted, click the **Shares** tab at the bottom of Failover Cluster Manager.

22. Take a screen shot of the Failover Cluster Manager by pressing **Alt+Prt Scr** and then paste it into your Lab 7 worksheet file in the page provided by pressing **Ctrl+V**.

End of exercise. Close all windows.

Lab Challenge	Designing a Failover Solution Project II
Overview	You are an administrator for the Contoso Corporation, which produces smart devices for the home. Read Appendix A for background information about the company and then read the information presented in this exercise.
Mindset	Since your company has grown, it is now more important to minimize downtime. In Lab 4, you developed a plan to create failover clusters out of some of the systems. In this exercise, you will modify the plan to include looking at file servers to determine which need to be General Use File Server clusters and which need to be Scale-Out File Server clusters.
Completion time	40 minutes

Create a proposal that includes the following sections:

- Purpose of the Project
- Requirements of the Project
- The Proposed Solution

When writing the proposal, you must explain the reasoning behind your choices.

End of lab. You can log off or start a different lab. If you want to restart this lab, you'll need to click the End Lab button in order for the lab to be reset.

LAB 8
PLANNING AND IMPLEMENTING A BUSINESS CONTINUITY AND DISASTER RECOVERY SOLUTION

THIS LAB CONTAINS THE FOLLOWING EXERCISES AND ACTIVITIES:

Exercise 8.1	Planning a Business Continuity and Disaster Recovery Solution
Exercise 8.2	Installing SQL Server Report Server
Exercise 8.3	Installing System Center 2012 R2 Data Protection Manager
Exercise 8.4	Configuring System Center Data Protection Manager
Exercise 8.5	Creating a Protection Group
Exercise 8.6	Performing a Backup and Restore with DPM
Lab Challenge	Designing a Backup and Recovery Plan

BEFORE YOU BEGIN

The lab environment consists of student workstations connected to a local area network, along with a server that functions as the domain controller for a domain called contoso.com. The computers required for this lab are listed in Table 8-1.

Table 8-1
Computers required for Lab 8

Computer	*Operating System*	*Computer Name*
Server	Windows Server 2012 R2	RWDC01
Server	Windows Server 2012 R2	Server01
Server	Windows Server 2012 R2	Server02
Server	Windows Server 2012 R2	Server03

In addition to the computers, you will also need the software listed in Table 8-2 to complete Lab 8.

Table 8-2
Software required for Lab 8

Software	*Location*
System Center 2012 R2 Data Protection Manager	\\rwdc01\software
Lab 8 student worksheet	Lab08_worksheet.docx (provided by instructor)

Working with Lab Worksheets

Each lab in this manual requires that you answer questions, shoot screen shots, and perform other activities that you will document in a worksheet named for the lab, such as Lab08_worksheet.docx. You will find these worksheets on the book companion site. It is recommended that you use a USB flash drive to store your worksheets, so you can submit them to your instructor for review. As you perform the exercises in each lab, open the appropriate worksheet file, fill in the required information, and then save the file to your flash drive.

SCENARIO

After completing this lab, you will be able to:

- Design and Plan a backup and recovery strategy
- Install SQL Server Report Server
- Install and configure System Center Data Protection Manager
- Create a Protection Group
- Perform a backup and restore using DPM
- Design a backup and recovery plan

Estimated lab time: 205 minutes

Exercise 8.1	Planning a Business Continuity and Disaster Recovery Solution
Overview	In this written exercise, you will read the background information for the Contoso Corporation found in Appendix A. You will then read the information introduced in this lesson and answer the questions.
Mindset	By now, you should understand the importance of backing up and recovering machines. Protecting your data and ensuring that your services, applications, and data are available during and after a disaster is extremely important. Therefore, as a system administrator, you need to plan for the worst disaster yet hope for the best outcome.
Completion time	20 minutes

Question 1	*What is the best method in data recovery?*

Question 2	*You are thinking about achieving 99.999% availability for your systems. What is the biggest factor in achieving the 5 nines?*

Question 3	*When providing resilience and high availability, what should each physical system use?*

Question 4	*Which type of servers should you use when you need to have redundant or highly available servers?*

Question 5	*You have a system with a single drive/volume. When performing a backup, what items need to be backed up if you are going to restore the system from scratch?*

Question 6	*You have a server with a large folder. You estimate that a normal backup would take about 30 hours. Which type of back up would you use if you need to ensure that you can recover a file from any specific day?*

Question 7	*You want to create a repository that will store weekly and daily backups for several months. Which application can be used to maintain the repository and perform the automatic backups and removal of old backups?*

Question 8	*You need to create a repository for shared folders and a repository for Active Directory. How many protection groups should you create?*

Question 9	*You want to create a warm site for a Data Recovery (DR) site. Within the DR site, you want to have a copy of some key systems that you can start if the primary data center becomes unavailable. What should you do?*

Exercise 8.2	Installing SQL Server Report Server
Overview	In this exercise, you will install the SQL Server Report Server on the same server that Operations Manager is installed.
Mindset	Operations Manager uses SQL Server Report Server (SSRS) to create, manage, and store reports. SSRS allows for the creation and retrieval of reports.
Completion time	40 minutes

1. On Server03, log on using the **contoso\administrator** account and the **Pa$$w0rd** password.
2. On the task bar, click the **File Explorer** icon. Then open the **\\rwdc01\software** folder.
3. Double-click the SQL Server 2012 with SP1 ISO file.
4. Double-click the **setup** application.
5. In the SQL Server Installation Center, click **Installation**.
6. Click **New SQL Server stand-alone installation or add features to an existing installation**.
7. In the SQL Server 2012 Setup wizard, on the Setup Support Rules page, click **OK**.
8. On the Product Updates page, immediately deselect the **Include SQL Server product updates** option and then click **Next**.

9. On the Setup Support Rules page, click **Next**. On the Installation Type page, click **Add features to an existing instance of SQL Server 2012** and then click **Next**.

10. On the Feature Selection page, select **Reporting Services – Native.**

11. Click **Next**.

12. On the Installation Rules page, click **Next**.

13. On the Disk Space Requirements page, click **Next**.

14. On the Server Configuration page, click **Next**.

15. On the Reporting Services Configuration page, click **Next**.

16. On the Error Reporting page, click **Next**.

17. On the Installation Configuration Rules page, click **Next**.

18. On the Ready to Install page, click **Install.**

19. Take a screen shot of the SQL Server 2012 Setup by pressing **Alt+Prt Scr** and then paste it into your Lab 8 worksheet file in the page provided by pressing **Ctrl+V**.

20. Click **Close.**

21. Click the **Start** button and then click the **Show All Applications** button (down arrow). Then under Microsoft SQL Server 2012, click **Reporting Services Configuration Manager**.

22. In the Reporting Services Configuration Manager, the Reporting Services Configuration Connection dialog box also opens. Click **Connect**.

23. Click **Web Service URL**.

Question 10	*What is the URL for Web Service?*

24. Click **Apply**.

25. Click **Database**.

26. Click **Change Database**.

27. In the Change Database page, on the Action page, Create a new report server database is already selected. Click **Next**.

28. On the Database Server page, for the Server Name, click **Next**.

29. On the Database page, for the Database Name text box, type **ReportServerDPM**. Click **Next**.

30. On the Credentials page, for the Authentication Type, select **Windows Credentials**. In the User name (Domain\user) text box, type **contoso\administrator**. For the Password text box, type **Pa$$w0rd**. Click **Next**.

31. On the Summary page, click **Next**. The installation will start and may take a couple of minutes.

32. When the database is configured, take a screen shot of the Report Server Database Configuration wizard by pressing **Alt+Prt Scr** and then paste it into your Lab 8 worksheet file in the page provided by pressing **Ctrl+V**.

33. Click **Finish**.

34. Click **Report Manager URL**.

Question 11	*What is the URL for Report Manager?*

35. Click **Apply**.

36. Click **Exit**.

37. Using Server Manager, open the **Services** console.

38. Double-click **SQL Server Agent (MSSQLSERVER)** service and click the **Log On** tab.

39. In the This account text box, type **contoso\administrator**. For the Password and Confirm password text boxes, type **Pa$$w0rd**. Click **OK**.

40. When a message indicates that the new logon name will not take effect until you stop and restart the service, click **OK**.

41. Right-click the **SQL Server Agent** (MSSQLSERVER) service and choose **Restart**.

42. Double-click **SQL Server Reporting Services (MSSQLSERVER)** service and click the **Log On** tab.

43. In the This account text box, type **contoso\administrator**. For the Password and Confirm password text boxes, type **Pa$$w0rd**. Click **OK twice**.

44. Right-click the **SQL Server Reporting Services (MSSQLSERVER)** service and choose **Restart**.

45. Click the **Start** button and then click the **Show All Applications** button (down arrow). Then under Microsoft SQL Server 2012, click **Reporting Services Configuration Manager**.

46. When you are prompted to connect to SERVER03, click **Connect**.

47. Click **Encryption Keys**.

48. In the Delete Encrypted Content section, click the **Delete** button. When you are prompted to confirm that you want to delete all encrypted data, click **Yes**.

49. Click the **Exit** button to close the Reporting Services Configuration Manager.

End of exercise. Close all windows.

Exercise 8.3	Installing System Center 2012 R2 Data Protection Manager
Overview	In this exercise, you will install System Center 2012 R2 Data Protection Manager.
Mindset	System Center 2012R2 Data Protection Manager (DPM) provides an advanced backup software package that allows for disk-based and tape-based data protection and recovery of servers, including Microsoft SQL Server, Exchange Server, SharePoint, virtual servers, and file servers. In addition, DPM also supports Windows desktops and laptops and can also centrally manage system state and Bare Metal Recovery.
Completion time	20 minutes

1. On Server03, log on using the **contoso\administrator** account and the **Pa$$w0rd** password.

2. Open File Explorer by clicking the File Explorer icon on the task bar. Open the **\\rwdc01\software** folder.

3. Perform one of the following:

   a. If you have a DPM ISO file, double-click the DPM ISO file. When the DVD drive opens, double-click **SCDPM** folder and then double-click the **Setup** application. On the Data Protection Manager splash screen, under Install, click **Data Protection Manager**.

   b. If you have the System Center 2012 R2 folder, double-click the **System Center 2012 R2** folder, double-click the **SC2012_R2-SCDPM_EVAL** compressed file and then double-click the **SC2012_R2_SCDPM_EVAL** application. Click **Extract All**. Click **Extract**. After extraction completes, open the **\\rwdc01\software\System Center 2012 R2\SC2012_R2-SCDPM_EVAL** folder. Double-click **SC2012_R2_SCDPM_EVAL**. When you are prompted to run the file, click **Run**. When the Welcome screen appears, click **Next**. On the Select Destination Location page, click **Next** and then click **Extract**. Click **Finish**. Open the **\\rwdc01\software\SC2012 R2 SCDPM\SCDPM** folder and, in the SCDPM subfolder, double-click the **Setup** application.

4. In the Data Protection Manager splash screen, under Install, click **Data Protection Manager**.

5. In the Microsoft Software License Terms dialog box, select the **I accept the license terms and conditions** option and then click **OK**.

6. In the Data Protection Manager Setup wizard, on the Welcome page, click **Next**.

Question 12	*Which versions of SQL server are supported by DPM?*

7. On the Prerequisite check page, the Use stand-alone SQL Server option is already selected. In the Instance of SQL Server text box, type **Server03**. Click one of the other text boxes and then click the **Check and Install** button. Click **Next**.

8. If a warning indicates the SISFilter was missing but has been installed, restart the computer and restart the DPM installation, beginning with the last sentence in Step 3b.

9. On the Production Registration page, in the Company text box, type **User**. In the Company text box, type **Company**. Click **Next**.

10. On the Installation Settings page, click **Next**.

11. On the Microsoft Update Opt-in page, select **I do not want to use Microsoft Update** and then click **Next**.

12. On the Customer Experience Improvement Program page, click **No, remind me later** and then click **Next**.

13. On the Summary of Settings page, click **Install**.

14. Take a screen shot of the Operations Manager console by pressing **Alt+Prt Scr** and then paste it into your Lab 8 worksheet file in the page provided by pressing **Ctrl+V**.

15. On the Installation page, when the installation is finished, click **Close**.

End of exercise. Close DPM installation program and folders.

Exercise 8.4	Configuring System Center Data Protection Manager
Overview	In this exercise, you will deploy and install the agent on systems that you want to protect with System Center Data Protection Manager.
Mindset	To perform backups using System Center Protection Manager, you have to install agents, which will guide the backups performed by DPM.
Completion time	15 minutes

1. On Server03, click the **Start** button, click the All Programs button (down arrow), and then click **Microsoft System Center 2012 R2 Data Protection Manager**.

2. In the System Center 2012 R2 DPM Administrator Console, click the **Management** workspace.

3. On the navigation bar, click **Install** on the ribbon.

4. In the Protection Agent Installation Wizard starts, select **Install agents** and then click **Next**.

5. On the Select Computers page, select all computers that are listed and then click **Add**. Click **Next**.

6. On the Enter Credentials page, in the User name box, type **Administrator**. In the Password text box, type **Pa$$w0rd**. Click **Next**.

7. On the Choose Restart Method page, click **Yes, Restart the selected computers after installing the protection agents (if required)** and then click **Next**.

8. On the Summary page, click **Install**.

9. Wait until the Results column shows a Success status for each server on which you installed the agent.

10. Take a screen shot of the Operations Manager console by pressing **Alt+Prt Scr** and then paste it into your Lab 8 worksheet file in the page provided by pressing **Ctrl+V**.

Question 13	*Why did the installation of the protection agent on Cluster01 fail?*

11. When the installation is complete, click **Close**.

End of exercise. Leave the System Center 2012 R2 DPM Administrator Console open for the following exercises.

Exercise 8.5	Creating a Protection Group
Overview	In this exercise, you will define and create protection groups in DPM.
Mindset	To automatically back up a folder, you can create a data protection group that specifies how often you want to create a recovery point. However, when you create a recovery point, you must ensure that you have plenty of disk space to hold all of the data. After the data protection group is created, you can create a recovery point any time.
Completion time	25 minutes

1. On Server02, log on using the **contoso\administrator** account and the **Pa$$w0rd** password.
2. On the taskbar, click the **File Explorer** icon. Then double-click the **Local Disk (C:)**.
3. Create a folder called **Data**.
4. Right-click the Data folder and choose **Properties**.
5. Click the **Sharing** tab.
6. Click the **Advanced Sharing** button.
7. In the Advanced Sharing dialog box, select the **Share this folder** option.
8. Click the **Permissions** button.
9. In the Permissions for Data dialog box, select the **Allow Full Control** checkbox for Everyone.
10. Click **OK** to close the Permissions for Data dialog box.
11. Click **OK** to close the Advanced Sharing dialog box.
12. Click **Close** to close the Data Properties dialog box.
13. Double-click the **Data** folder.
14. Create a text file called **testdoc.txt**. In the file, place your name and save the document.
15. On Server03, using Server Manager, click **Tools** > **Computer Management**.
16. In the Computer Management console, under **Storage**, click **Disk Management**.
17. Right-click **Disk 1** and choose **Online**.
18. Right-click **Disk 1** and choose **Initialize Disk**. In the Initialize Disk dialog box, click **OK**.
19. Close **Computer Management**.
20. On Server03, go back to the **System Center 2012 R2 DPM Administrator Console** and click the **Management** workspace.
21. Click **Disks**. Then in the ribbon, click **Add**.
22. Select **Disk 1** and then click **Add**. Click **OK**. When you are prompted to convert the disk to dynamic disks, click **Yes**.
23. On Server03, click the **Protection** workspace.

24. On the ribbon, click **New**.

25. In the Create New Protection Group Wizard, on the Welcome page, click **Next**.

26. On the Select Protection Group Type page, select **Servers** and then click **Next**.

27. On the Select Group Members page, under Available members, expand the **Server02**, expand **All Shares**, and then select **Data**, click **OK**.

28. When you receive a warning about protecting the system volume system state, click **OK**.

29. Back on the Select Group Members page, click **Next**.

30. On the Select Data Protection Method, answer the following question and then click **Next**.

Question 14	*What is the name of the Protection group?*

31. On the Select short-term goals page, answer the following questions. Click **Next**.

Question 15	*What times are the recovery points?*

32. On the Review Disk Allocation page, click **Next**.

33. On the Choose Replica Creation Method page, click **Next**.

34. On the Consistency check options, click **Next**.

35. On the Summary page, click **Create Group**.

36. When the protection groups is created, take a screen shot of the Create New Protection Group window by pressing **Alt+Prt Scr** and then paste it into your Lab 8 worksheet file in the page provided by pressing **Ctrl+V**.

37. Click **Close** to close Create New Protection Group Status window.

End of exercise. Leave the System Center 2012 R2 DPM Administrator Console open for the following exercises.

Exercise 8.6	Performing a Backup and Restore with DPM
Overview	In this exercise, you will perform a backup and restore using DPM.
Mindset	When you create a protection group, you can specify how often a backup will occur. However, if necessary, you can manually perform a backup at any time and perform a restore as needed. When you perform a restore, you can restore files back to the original location or to a new location so that you don't overwrite the current file.
Completion time	20 minutes

1. On Server03, using the System Center 2012 R2 Administrator Console, click the **Protection Workspace**.
2. Click the **Protection Group 1** and then right-click **\\server02.contoso.com\Data** and choose **Create recovery point**.
3. In the Create recovery point dialog box, with the **Create a recovery point after synchronizing** selected, click **OK**.
4. When the recovery point is created, take a screen shot of the Create Recovery Point dialog box by pressing **Alt+Prt Scr** and then paste it into your Lab 8 worksheet file in the page provided by pressing **Ctrl+V**.
5. Click **Close**.
6. Click the Recovery workspace.
7. In the left pane, select **contoso.com\Server02\All Protected Volumes\C:**. Then under Recovery points for: Recoverable Data, select today's date. In the bottom pane, double-click **Data**.
8. Right-click the **testdoc.txt** file and choose **Recover**.
9. In the Recovery Wizard, on the Review Recovery Selection page, click **Next**.
10. On the Select recovery type page, select Recovery to the original location option and then click **Next**.

Question 16	*Why would you not want to recovery to its original location?*

11. On the Specify Recovery Options page, click **Next**.
12. On the Summary page, click **Recover**.

13. Take a screen shot of the Recovery Wizard by pressing **Alt+Prt Scr** and then paste it into your Lab 8 worksheet file in the page provided by pressing **Ctrl+V**.

14. Click **Close**.

15. Click **Protection** workspace.

16. Right-click the **server02.contoso.com\Data share** and choose **Stop protection of member**.

17. In the Stop Protection – Protection Group 1 dialog box, click **Stop Protection**.

18. Click **Close**.

End of exercise. Close all windows.

Lab Challenge	Designing a Backup and Recovery Plan
Overview	You are an administrator for the Contoso Corporation, which produces smart devices for the home. Read Appendix A for background information about the company and then read the information presented in this exercise.
Mindset	You need to develop backup and recovery plans for the Contoso Corporation. Therefore, you need to figure out what needs to be backed up, the method to use to perform the backups, and how often to back up.
Completion time	65 minutes

Create a proposal that includes the following sections:

- Purpose of the Project
- Requirements of the Project
- The Proposed Solution

When writing the proposal, you must explain the reasoning behind your choices.

End of lab. You can log off or start a different lab. If you want to restart this lab, you'll need to click the End Lab button in order for the lab to be reset.

LAB 9 PLANNING AND IMPLEMENTING VIRTUALIZATION HOSTS

THIS LAB CONTAINS THE FOLLOWING EXERCISES AND ACTIVITIES:

Exercise 9.1	Planning Virtualization Hosts
Exercise 9.2	Installing and Configuring VMM
Lab Challenge	Designing Virtualization Project I

BEFORE YOU BEGIN

The lab environment consists of student workstations connected to a local area network, along with a server that functions as the domain controller for a domain called contoso.com. The computers required for this lab are listed in Table 9-1.

Table 9-1
Computers required for Lab 9

Computer	*Operating System*	*Computer Name*
Server	Windows Server 2012 R2	RWDC01
Server	Windows Server 2012 R2	Server01
Server	Windows Server 2012 R2	Server03
Server	Windows Server 2012 R2	VServer01
Server	Windows Server 2012 R2	VServer02

In addition to the computers, you will also need the software listed in Table 9-2 to complete Lab 9.

Table 9-2
Software required for Lab 9

Software	*Location*
System Center 2012 R2 Virtual Machine Manager	\\rwdc01\software
Lab 9 student worksheet	Lab09_worksheet.docx (provided by instructor)

Working with Lab Worksheets

Each lab in this manual requires that you answer questions, shoot screen shots, and perform other activities that you will document in a worksheet named for the lab, such as Lab09_worksheet.docx. You will find these worksheets on the book companion site. It is recommended that you use a USB flash drive to store your worksheets, so you can submit them to your instructor for review. As you perform the exercises in each lab, open the appropriate worksheet file, fill in the required information, and then save the file to your flash drive.

SCENARIO

After completing this lab, you will be able to:

- Plan and design a VMM deployment
- Install VMM
- Add hosts to VMM

Estimated lab time: 130 minutes

Exercise 9.1	Planning Virtualization Hosts
Overview	In this written exercise, you will read the background information for the Contoso Corporation found in Appendix A. You will then read the information introduced in this lesson and answer the questions.
Mindset	The Microsoft System Center product line provides management and report tools designed for management of large number of computers. System Center 2012 R2 Virtual Machine Manager (VMM) enables centralized management of virtualized workloads. VMM allows you to manage the virtualized data center infrastructure, increase physical server utilization (including providing simple and fast consolidation of the virtual infrastructure), and perform intelligent workplace placement based on performance data and user-defined business policies.
Completion time	10 minutes

Question 1	*For the Contoso Corporation, how many VMM management servers do you need?*

Question 2	*What kind of SQL server do you need for VMM?*

Question 3	*How many VMM consoles should you install?*

Question 4	*Which systems can the VMM console run on?*

Question 5	*What is used to create a central repository for templates and ISO files that can be used by multiple hosts?*

Exercise 9.2	Installing and Configuring VMM
Overview	In this exercise, you will install System Center 2012 R2 Virtual Machine Manager (VMM).
Mindset	VMM enables centralized management of virtualized workloads and allows you to manage the virtualized data center infrastructure and increase physical server utilization (including providing simple and fast consolidation of the virtual infrastructure).
Completion time	60 minutes

1. Log on to **Server01** server using the **contoso\administrator** account and the password **Pa$$w0rd**.

2. On Server01, using File Explorer, open the **RWDC01\Software** folder.

3. Double-click the **SQLCmdLnUtils** application. When you are prompted to confirm that you want to run this file, click **Run**.

4. In the Microsoft SQL Server 2012 Command Line Utilities Wizard, on the Welcome page, click **Next**.

5. On the License Agreement page, **select I accept the terms in the license agreement** and click **Next**.

6. On the Ready to Install the Program page, click **Install**.

7. When the utilities are installed, click **Finish**.

8. Perform one of the following:

   a. From the \\RWDC01\Software folder, if you have the System Center 2012 R2 VMM ISO file, double-click the System Center 2012 R2 VMM ISO file.

   b. If you have the System Center 2012 R2 folder, double-click the System Center 2012 R2 folder. Double-click **SC2012_R2_SCVMM (VirtualMachineManager)**. In the SC2012 R2 SCVMM Wizard, click **Next**. On the Select Destination Location page, click **Next**. On the Ready to **Extract** page, click **Extract**. **Click Finish**. Then open the \\rwdc01\software\SC2012 R2 SCVMM folder.

9. Double-click **setup.exe**.

10. On the Microsoft System Center 2012 R2 Virtual Machine Manager splash screen, click **Install**.

11. When a message displays, indicating Microsoft Visual C++ 2010 Redistributed Package was successfully installed and that the system needs to be rebooted, click **OK** and then reboot Server01.

12. Log on to **Server01** using the **contoso\Administrator** account and the password **Pa$$w0rd**.

13. Go back to \\rwdc01\software\SC2012 R2 SCVMM and double-click the **setup.exe**.

14. On the Microsoft System Center 2012 R2 Virtual Machine Manager splash screen, click **Install**.

15. In the Microsoft System Center 2012 R2 Virtual Machine Manager Setup Wizard, on the Select features to install page, click **VMM management server** and **VMM console**. Click **Next**.

16. On the Product registration information page, click **Next**.

17. On the Please read this license agreement page, click **I have read, understood, and agree with the terms of the license agreement** and then click **Next**.

18. On the Customer Experience Improvement Program (CEIP) page, click **No, I am not willing to participate** and then click **Next**.

19. On the Microsoft Update page, Select **Off**. Click **Next**.

20. On the Installation location page, click **Next**.

21. On the Prerequisite page, click **Next**.

22. On the Database configuration page, for the Server name text box, type **Server03**. Then click the New database text box.

Question 6	*What is the default name of the database?*

23. Click **Next**.

24. On the Configure service account and distributed key management page, Domain account is already selected. In the Username and domain text box, type **contoso\administrator**. In the Password text box, type **Pa$$w0rd**.

Question 7	*What do you need to do if you want to make VMM highly available?*

25. Select the **Store my keys in Active Directory** option. In the Provide the location in Active Directory text box, type **CN=DKM,DC=contoso,DC=com.** Click **Next**.

26. On the Port configuration page, answer the following question and then click **Next**.

Question 8	*Which port is used by the VMM console?*

27. On the Library configuration page, Create a new library share is already selected. Answer the following question and then click **Next**.

Question 9	*What is the location of the MSSCVMMLibrary library share?*

28. On the Installation summary page, click **Install**. This will take a few minutes to install.

29. When VMM is installed successfully, take a screen shot of the Microsoft System Center 2012 R2 Virtual Machine Manager Setup Wizard by pressing **Alt+Prt Scr** and then paste it into your Lab 9 worksheet file in the page provided by pressing **Ctrl+V**.

30. Deselect **Check for the latest Virtual Machine Manager updates** and then click **Close.**

31. In the Connect to Server dialog box, click **Connect**. Virtual Machine Manager opens.

32. In the Connect to Server dialog box, select **Automatically connect with these settings** and then click **Connect**.

33. Take a screen shot of the Virtual Machine Manager Setup Wizard by pressing **Alt+Prt Scr** and then paste it into your Lab 9 worksheet file in the page provided by pressing **Ctrl+V**.

34. Log in to **RWDC01** with the username of **contoso\administrator** with the password of **Pa$$w0rd**.

35. Open **Active Directory Users and Computers**. Create a domain account named **HyperVAdmin** with the password of **Pa$$w0rd**. Make the HyperVAdmin a domain administrator. Configure the password to never expire.

36. Go back to **Server01**. In the Virtual Machine Manager, open the **Fabric** workspace. Then expand the **Servers** node and click **All Hosts**.

37. Right-click **All Hosts** and choose **Add Hyper-V Hosts and Clusters**.

38. In the Add Resource Wizard, on the Resource Location page, Windows Server computers in a trusted Active Directory domain is already selected. Click **Next**.

39. On the Credentials page, Use an existing Run As account is already selected. Click the **Browse** button.

40. In the Select a Run As Account dialog box, click the **Create Run As Account** button.

41. In the Create Run As Account dialog box, for the Name text box and the User name text box, type **contoso\hypervadmin**. For the Password text box and the Confirm password text box, type **Pa$$w0rd**. Click **OK**.

42. Back on the Select a Run As Account dialog box, click **OK**.

43. Back on the Credentials page, click **Next**.

44. On the Discovery Scope page, Specify Windows Server computers by names is already selected. In the Computer names text box, type the following and then click **Next**.

    VServer01

    VServer02

45. On the Target resources page, click the **Select All** button and then click **Next**.

46. On the Host Settings page, select **Reassociate this host with this VMM environment** and then click **Next**.

47. On the Summary page, click **Finish**.

48. When the Jobs window opens, if the virtual machine host fails, reboot Vserver01 and VServer02. Then in the Jobs window, highlight both the Add virtual machine host Failed entries and click **Restart**. When you are prompted to restart the selected jobs, click **Yes**. In the Restart Job dialog box, click **Browse** and then double-click **contoso\HyperVAdmin**. Click **OK** to close the Restart Job dialog box.

49. Wait a few minutes for the servers to finish. When the host has been added, close the **Jobs** window.

50. Take a screen shot of the All Hosts node by pressing **Alt+Prt Scr** and then paste it into your Lab 9 worksheet file in the page provided by pressing **Ctrl+V**.

    Leave Virtual Machine Manager open for the next exercise.

Lab Challenge	Designing Virtualization Project I
Overview	You are an administrator for the Contoso Corporation, which produces smart devices for the home. Read Appendix A for background information about the company and then read the information presented in this exercise.
Mindset	The Contoso Corporation has several servers running Hyper-V. You need to plan out the VMM deployment and virtual environment.
Completion time	60 minutes

Create a proposal that includes the following sections:

- Purpose of the Project
- Requirements of the Project
- The Proposed Solution

When writing the proposal, you must explain the reasoning behind your choices.

End of lab. You can log off or start a different lab. If you want to restart this lab, you'll need to click the End Lab button in order for the lab to be reset.

LAB 10
PLANNING AND IMPLEMENTING VIRTUAL MACHINES

THIS LAB CONTAINS THE FOLLOWING EXERCISES AND ACTIVITIES:

Exercise 10.1	Planning Virtual Machines
Exercise 10.2	Creating a Virtual Machine
Exercise 10.3	Configuring Memory Usage
Exercise 10.4	Configuring Placement
Lab Challenge	Designing Virtualization Project II

BEFORE YOU BEGIN

The lab environment consists of student workstations connected to a local area network, along with a server that functions as the domain controller for a domain called contoso.com. The computers required for this lab are listed in Table 10-1.

Table 10-1
Computers required for Lab 10

Computer	*Operating System*	*Computer Name*
Server	Windows Server 2012 R2	RWDC01
Server	Windows Server 2012 R2	Server01
Server	Windows Server 2012 R2	Server03
Server	Windows Server 2012 R2	VServer01
Server	Windows Server 2012 R2	VServer02

In addition to the computers, you will also need the software listed in Table 10-2 to complete Lab 10.

Table 10-2
Software required for Lab 10

Software	*Location*
Lab 10 student worksheet	Lab10_worksheet.docx (provided by instructor)

Working with Lab Worksheets

Each lab in this manual requires that you answer questions, shoot screen shots, and perform other activities that you will document in a worksheet named for the lab, such as Lab10_worksheet.docx. You will find these worksheets on the book companion site. It is recommended that you use a USB flash drive to store your worksheets, so you can submit them to your instructor for review. As you perform the exercises in each lab, open the appropriate worksheet file, fill in the required information, and then save the file to your flash drive.

SCENARIO

After completing this lab, you will be able to:

- Plan and design virtual machine configuration and deployment
- Create a virtual machine using VMM
- Configure VM memory usage
- Configure VM placement

Estimated lab time: 100 minutes

Exercise 10.1	Planning Virtual Machines
Overview	In this written exercise, you will read the background information for the Contoso Corporation found in Appendix A. You will then read the information introduced in this lesson and answer the questions.
Mindset	When planning VMs, remember that VMs are virtual machines that run on physical hosts. This section covers steps that you can perform to make the physical host highly available, which will, in turn, help make the virtual machines highly available..
Completion time	15 minutes

Question 1	*What are the storage requirements when creating highly available virtual machines?*

Question 2	*What other way can you create a highly available virtual machine without using host or guest clustering?*

Question 3	*If your Hyper-V environment is near capacity, how can you ensure that critical machines have sufficient memory before other machines?*

Question 4	*Which option should be used to ensure that two servers that make up a failover cluster are on two different Hyper-V switches?*

Question 5	*Which option should be used to place a server on a particular Hyper-V host that is part of a Hyper-V cluster?*

Question 6	*Which options should be configured to ensure that virtual machines are distributed equally between Hyper-V hosts?*

Question 7	*You need to deploy 20 web servers (virtual machines) running on a Hyper-V environment. Each of the virtual machines is identical. What is the best way to create and deploy the virtual machines?*

Exercise 10.2	Creating a Virtual Machine
Overview	In this exercise, you will create two virtual machines using VMM.
Mindset	By deploying virtual machines with VMM, you can easily deploy virtual machines to any host and provide enterprise functionality such as high availability that was not available on Hyper-V by itself.
Completion time	15 minutes

1. On Server01, log on using the **contoso\administrator** account and the **Pa$$w0rd** password.
2. Using the **Start** button, start the **Virtual Machine Manager**.
3. Click the **VMs and Services** workspace.
4. Expand the **All Hosts** node and then expand **Cluster01** node.
5. Right-click **VServer01** and choose **Create Virtual Machine**.
6. In the Create Virtual Machine Wizard, select the **Create the new virtual machine with a blank virtual hard disk** option and then click **Next**.
7. On the Identity page, in the Virtual machine name text box, type **VM3**. Click **Next**.
8. On the Configure Hardware page, answer the following question and then click **Next**.

Question 8	*How big is the disk and what type of disk is it?*

Question 9	*What is the processor and memory set to?*

9. Click the **VM3_disk_1** disk (found under IDE Devices).
10. Change the size (GB) to **5**.
11. Click **Availability** (found under Advanced). Select **Make this virtual machine highly available** and then click **Next**.
12. On the Select Destination page, the Place the virtual machine on a host option is selected and the Destination is set to All Hosts. Click **Next**.
13. On the Select Host page, select **VServer01** and then click **Next**.

14. On the Configure Settings page, answer the following question and then click **Next**.

Question 10	*Where is the VM going to be created?*

15. On the Select Networks page, click **Next**.

16. On the Add Properties page, answer the following question and then click **Next**.

Question 11	*Which operating system is specified?*

17. On the Summary page, click **Create**.

18. When the VM is created, close the Jobs window.

19. Take a screen shot of the VMs listed in Virtual Machine Manager by pressing **Alt+Prt Scr** and then paste it into your Lab 10 worksheet file in the page provided by pressing **Ctrl+V**.

20. Repeat the process and create a VM4.

End of exercise. Leave Virtual Machine Manager open for the next exercise.

Exercise 10.3	Configuring Memory Usage
Overview	In this exercise, you will configure the memory usage used by a virtual machine.
Mindset	When you create a virtual machine, you define startup RAM, which is the amount of memory that a virtual machine will use when the computer boots and it represents the minimum amount of physical memory the virtual machine will use. When specifying startup RAM, be sure that the startup RAM for all VMs does not exceed the physical RAM installed on the server. If you do exceed the physical RAM on the server, you need to remove some of the virtual machines or add memory to the host.
Completion time	10 minutes

1. On Server01, using the Virtual Machine Manager console, click the **VMs and Services** workspace.

2. Expand the **All Hosts** node, expand the **Cluster01** node, and then click **vserver01**.

3. Right-click **VM1** and choose **Properties**.

4. Click **Hardware Configuration**.

Question 12	*How many processors and memory is assigned to VM1?*

5. Click the **Memory** option.

6. Select the **Dynamic** option.

7. Configure the following:

   Startup memory: **64 MB**

   Minimum memory: **64 MB**

8. Take a screen shot of the memory options by pressing **Alt+Prt Scr** and then paste it into your Lab 10 worksheet file in the page provided by pressing **Ctrl+V**.

9. Scroll down and click **Memory Weight**.

Question 13	*What is the memory weight set to?*

10. To close the VM1 Properties dialog box, click **OK**.

End of exercise. Leave Virtual Machine Manager open for the next exercise.

Exercise 10.4	Configuring Placement
Overview	In this exercise, you will configure preferred hosts and availability sets with Virtual Machine Manager.
Mindset	In larger organizations with multiple physical host machines, administrators often want to control which physical host a particular VM will run on. In some cases, administrators might want to have certain VMs run on different machines. Therefore, this section discusses how to place certain virtual machines on physical hosts.
Completion time	15 minutes

1. On Server01, using Virtual Machine Manager, click the **VMs and Services** workspace.

2. Navigate to VServer01. In the results pane, right-click the **VM3** and choose **Properties**.

3. When the VM3 Properties dialog box opens, click the **Settings** option on the left.

Question 14	*What are the possible owners for VM3?*

4. Under Preferred Owner, select **vserver02.contoso.com** and then **click Move Up**.
5. Click **OK** to close the VM3 Properties dialog box.
6. Right-click **VM3** and choose **Properties**.
7. In the VM3 Properties dialog box, click **Hardware Configuration** and then click **Availability**.
8. Under Availability sets, click **Manage availability sets**.
9. In the Manage Availability Sets dialog box, click **Create**.
10. In the Create Availability Set dialog box, in the Name text box, type **FailOverCluster1** and then click **OK**. Click **OK** to close VM3 Properties.
11. Wait about 30 seconds, then right-click **VM4** and choose **Properties**.
12. In the VM4 Properties dialog box, click **Hardware Configuration** and then click **Availability**.
13. Under Availability sets, click **Manage availability sets**.
14. Click **FailoverCluster1** and then click **Add**.
15. To close the Manage Availability Sets dialog box, click **OK**.
16. Click **OK** to close the VM4 Properties dialog box.
17. Expand the **Availability Set Name** column.
18. Take a screen shot of VMs showing the Availability Set Name column by pressing **Alt+Prt Scr** and then paste it into your Lab 10 worksheet file in the page provided by pressing **Ctrl+V**.

End of exercise. Close all windows.

Lab Challenge	Designing Virtualization Project II
Overview	You are an administrator for the Contoso Corporation, which produces smart devices for the home. Read Appendix A for background information about the company and then read the information presented in this exercise.
Mindset	Now that you have implemented VMM with your Hyper-V environment, you now need to plan and design your virtual machine deployments. In reviewing your plans for the previous labs, you need to consider how you can use VMM with Hyper-V to get the most out of your virtual environment.
Completion time	45 minutes

Modify the project plan that you started in Lab 9 by adding the planning and designing of virtual machines used with the Contoso Corporation. As stated before, the proposal should include the following sections: Create a proposal that includes the following sections:

- Purpose of the Project
- Requirements of the Project
- The Proposed Solution

When writing the proposal, you must explain the reasoning behind your choices.

End of lab. You can log off or start a different lab. If you want to restart this lab, you'll need to click the End Lab button in order for the lab to be reset.

LAB 11
PLANNING AND IMPLEMENTING VIRTUALIZATION NETWORKING

THIS LAB CONTAINS THE FOLLOWING EXERCISES AND ACTIVITIES:

Exercise 11.1	Planning Virtual Networks
Exercise 11.2	Creating a VMM Template
Exercise 11.3	Creating Virtual Networks
Exercise 11.4	Configuring an IP Pool
Exercise 11.5	Configuring MAC Address Settings
Lab Challenge	Designing Virtualization Project III

BEFORE YOU BEGIN

The lab environment consists of student workstations connected to a local area network, along with a server that functions as the domain controller for a domain called contoso.com. The computers required for this lab are listed in Table 11-1.

Table 11-1
Computers required for Lab 11

Computer	*Operating System*	*Computer Name*
Server	Windows Server 2012 R2	RWDC01
Server	Windows Server 2012 R2	Server01
Server	Windows Server 2012 R2	Server03
Server	Windows Server 2012 R2	VServer01
Server	Windows Server 2012 R2	VServer02

In addition to the computers, you will also need the software listed in Table 11-2 to complete Lab 11.

Table 11-2
Software required for Lab 11

Software	*Location*
Lab 11 student worksheet	Lab11_worksheet.docx (provided by instructor)

Working with Lab Worksheets

Each lab in this manual requires that you answer questions, shoot screen shots, and perform other activities that you will document in a worksheet named for the lab, such as Lab11_worksheet.docx. You will find these worksheets on the book companion site. It is recommended that you use a USB flash drive to store your worksheets, so you can submit them to your instructor for review. As you perform the exercises in each lab, open the appropriate worksheet file, fill in the required information, and then save the file to your flash drive.

SCENARIO

After completing this lab, you will be able to:

- Plan and design virtual networks
- Create VM templates
- Configure an IP pool
- Configure MAC address settings

Estimated lab time: 160 minutes

Exercise 11.1	Planning Virtual Networks
Overview	In this written exercise, you will read the background information for the Contoso Corporation found in Appendix A. You will then read the information introduced in this lesson and answer the questions.
Mindset	In VMM, you can create logical networks that can easily connect virtual machines to a network used for a particular function in your environment, such as the back-end, front-end, or a backup network. Logical networks would define IP subnets and, if needed, the virtual local area networks (VLANs).
Completion time	20 minutes

Question 1	*You need to design the networks that will be used with your virtual environment. For the Contoso Corporation, how many physical networks would you create and for what purpose?*

Question 2	*What is defined when you define logical networks?*

Question 3	*While you have a DHCP server for the clients, you do not have a DHCP server for the servers. What can you do to give you temporary IP addresses to new servers?*

Question 4	*Since the Contoso Corporation is using Hyper-V, how many MAC address pools do you need to create?*

Question 5	*Your manager is looking at expanding the company services by providing servers for clients. Which technology can be used to provide access to those virtual machines while isolating the other virtual machines from the clients?*

Question 6	*You have an application server and a database server that requires heavy traffic between the two. How can you ensure that this traffic does not hamper communications between other hosts?*

Question 7	*You want to ensure that a sever can only communicate with the Internet, and no other servers. What can you do?*

Question 8	*You are going to be adding VoIP to your corporation. What should be used to ensure VoIP phone calls are clear?*

Exercise 11.2	Creating a VMM Template
Overview	In this exercise, you will create a VMM Template. You will then deploy a new virtual machine with the template.
Mindset	VM templates are used to create new virtual machines and configure tiers in a service template. You can create a VM template based on an existing VM template or based on an existing virtual hard disk that is stored in a library.
Completion time	25 minutes

1. On Server01, log on using the **contoso\administrator** account and the **Pa$$w0rd** password.
2. Using Server Manager, open the **Services** console.
3. Right-click **System Center Virtual Machine Manager** and choose **Stop**.
4. To install the System Center 2012 R2 VMM Update Rollup 4, open **rwdc01\software** and double-click **kb2992024_vmmserver_amd64**. When you are prompted to confirm that you want to close the applications, click **OK**.
5. After the SCVMM Server is configured (which might take several minutes), reboot Server01.
6. On Server01, log on using the **contoso\administrator** account and the **Pa$$w0rd** password.
7. Open the **Virtual Machine Manager** console and then click the **Library** workspace.
8. Navigate to **Library\Library Servers\Server01.contoso.com\MSSCVMMLibrary\VHDs**. Click one of the blank disks. Then right-click the VHDs node and choose **Refresh**. Make sure the Status of the disks are OK. Note: The kb2992024_vmmserver_amd64 update fixes a bug related to these disks being offline.
9. Click **Templates**.
10. On the Home tab, in the Create group, click **Create VM Template**.

11. In the Create VM Template Wizard, on the Select Source page, click **Use an existing VM template or a virtual hard disk stored in the library** and then click **Browse**.

12. In the Select VM Template Source dialog box, click **Blank Disk – Small.vhdx**, click **OK**, and then click **Next**.

13. On the Identity page, in the VM Template name text box, type **VMTemplate01**. Click **Next**.

14. On the Configure Hardware page, click **Next**.

15. On the Configure Operating System page, for the Guest OS profile, select **Create new Windows operating system customization settings**.

Question 9	*Which operating system is already specified?*

16. Click **Next**.

17. On the Application configuration page, click **Next**.

18. On the SQL Server Configuration page, click **Next**.

19. On the Summary page, click **Create**.

20. When the Jobs window opens, close the Jobs window.

21. Take a screen shot of the Template node by pressing **Alt+Prt Scr** and then paste it into your Lab 11 worksheet file in the page provided by pressing **Ctrl+V**.

22. Click the **VMs and Services** workspace. Right-click **vserver01** and choose **Create Virtual Machine**.

23. In the Create Virtual Machine Wizard, on the Select Source page, click **Browse**. In the Select Virtual Machine Source dialog box, select **VMTemplate01** and then click **OK**.

24. Back on the Select Source page, click **Next**.

25. On the Identity page, on the Virtual machine name text box, type **VM5** and then click **Next**.

26. On the Configure Hardware page, under Advanced, click **Availability**. Select **Make this virtual machine highly available** and then click **Next**.

27. On the Configure Operating System page, click **Next**.

28. On the Select Destination page, click **Next**.

29. On the Select Host page, select **vserver01.contoso.com** and then click **Next**.

30. On the Configure Settings page, in the Computer name text box, type **VM5** and then click **Next**.

31. On the Select Networks page, click **Next**.

32. On the Add Properties page, click **Next**.

33. On the Summary page, click **Create**.

34. When the virtual machine is created, close the Jobs window. Ignore the error because the disk is not a bootable disk.

35. Click the VMs and Services workspace and take a screen shot of the Cluster01 showing the VMs Properties dialog box by pressing **Alt+Prt Scr** and then paste it into your Lab 11 worksheet file in the page provided by pressing **Ctrl+V**.

Leave Virtual Machine Manager open for the next exercise.

Exercise 11.3	Creating Virtual Networks
Overview	In this exercise, you will create a logical network and logical switch.
Mindset	When you configure networking using VMM, you need to provision network resources efficiently for a virtualized environment. This includes creating and defining logical networks, assigning static IP addresses and MAC addresses, and integrating load balancing.
Completion time	30 minutes

1. On Server01, in the VMM console, click the **Fabric** workspace.

2. On the Home tab, in the Show group, click **Fabric Resources**.

3. In the Fabric pane, expand **Networking** and then click **Logical Networks**.

4. In the Create group, click **Create Logical Network**.

5. In the Create Logical Network Wizard, on the Name page, in the Name text box, type **Network1** and then click **Next**.

6. On the Network Site page, click **Add** and then select **All Hosts**.

7. Click **Insert row**, click Enter IP subnet, type **192.168.1.0/24**, and then click **Next**.

8. On the Summary page, click **Finish**.

9. When the network is created, close the Jobs window.

10. Take a screen shot of the Logical Networks node by pressing **Alt+Prt Scr** and then paste it into your Lab 11 worksheet file in the page provided by pressing **Ctrl+V**.

11. In the Fabric pane, under Networking, click **Logical Switches**.

12. Click **Create** and then click **Hyper-V Port Profile**.

13. In the Create Hyper-V Port Profile dialog box, in the Name text box, type **Standard Profile**.

14. Select the Uplink Port profile option and then click **Next**.

15. On the Network Configuration, click **Network1_0** and then click **Next**.

16. On the Summary page, click **Finish**.

17. Close the Jobs dialog box.

18. On the Home tab, in the Create group, click **Create Logical Switch**.

19. In the Create Logical Switch Wizard, on the Getting Started page, click **Next**.

20. On the General page, in the Name text box, type **Switch01** and then click **Next**.

21. On the Extensions page, click **Next**.

22. On the Uplink page, click **Add**.

Question 10	*Which port profile is already selected?*

23. On the Add Uplink Port Profile dialog box, click **OK**. Click **Next**.

24. On the Virtual Port page, click **Next**.

25. On the Summary page, review and confirm the settings and then click **Finish**.

26. Close the Jobs dialog box.

27. Take a screen shot of the Logical Switches node by pressing **Alt+Prt Scr** and then paste it into your Lab 11 worksheet file in the page provided by pressing **Ctrl+V**.

28. On the VMM console, click the **VMs and Services** workspace.

29. On the Home tab, in the VMs and Services pane, in the Show group, click the **VM Networks** node.

30. On the Home tab, in the Create group, click **Create VM Network**.

31. In the Create VM Network Wizard, on the Name page, type **VMNetwork01** and then click **Next**.

32. On the Summary page, review the summary and then click **Finish**.

33. Close the Jobs window.

34. Take a screen shot of the VM Networks node by pressing **Alt+Prt Scr** and then paste it into your Lab 11 worksheet file in the page provided by pressing **Ctrl+V**.

35. In the Fabric pane, expand **Servers**, expand **All Hosts**, and then click **Cluster01**. In the Hosts pane, click **vserver01.contoso.com**.

36. On the Host tab, in the Properties group, click **Properties**.

37. In the vserver01.contoso.com Properties dialog box, click the **Virtual Switches** tab.

38. On the Virtual Switches tab, click **New Virtual Switch** and then click **New Logical Switch**.

39. Take a screen shot of the vserver01.contoso.com Properties dialog box by pressing **Alt+Prt Scr** and then paste it into your Lab 11 worksheet file in the page provided by pressing **Ctrl+V**.

40. Click **OK** to close the vserver01.contoso.com Properties dialog box. When you are prompted to confirm that you want to continue, click **OK**.

41. Right-click **vserver02.contoso.com** and choose **Properties**.

42. Click the **Virtual Switches** tab.

43. On the Virtual Switches tab, click **New Virtual Switch** and then click **New Logical Switch**.

44. Click **OK** to close the vserver02.contoso.com Properties dialog box. When you are prompted to confirm that you want to continue, click **OK**.

Leave Virtual Machine Manager open for the next exercise.

Exercise 11.4	Configuring an IP Pool
Overview	In this exercise, you will create an IP pool in Virtual Machine Manager.
Mindset	An IP pool can be used to assign IP configuration to those virtual machines without using a DHCP server.
Completion time	15 minutes

1. On Server01, In the **Fabric** workspace, expand **Networking** and then click **Logical Networks**.

2. On the Home tab, in the Show group, click **Fabric Resources**. In the Logical Networks and IP Pools pane, click **Network1**.

3. On the Home tab, in the Create group, click **Create > Create IP Pool**.

4. In the Create Static IP Address Pool Wizard, on the Name page, in the Name text box, type **IPPool01**.

Question 11	*Which logical network is selected?*

5. Click **Next**.

6. On the Network Site page, click **Next.**

7. On the IP address range, for the Starting IP address, type **192.168.1.201**.

8. Under VIPs and reserved IP addresses, specify IP address ranges that you want to reserve, such as a range for load balancer virtual IP addresses (VIPs). Click **Next**.

9. On the Gateway page, click **Insert**. Click **Enter gateway address** and then type **192.168.1.1**. Click **Next**.

10. On the DNS page, next to DNS Server Address, click **Insert**. Click **Enter DNS server address** and then type **192.168.1.50**.

11. For the Connection specific DNS suffix box, type **contoso.com**.

12. For the DNS Suffix, click **Insert**. Click **Enter DNS suffix** and then type **contoso.com**. Click **Next**.

13. On the WINS page, click **Next**.

14. On the Summary page, click **Finish**.

15. Close the Jobs dialog box.

16. Take a screen shot of the Logical Networks and IP Pools pane by pressing **Alt+Prt Scr** and then paste it into your Lab 11 worksheet file in the page provided by pressing **Ctrl+V**.

    Leave Virtual Machine Manager open for the next exercise.

Exercise 11.5	Configuring MAC Address Settings
Overview	In this exercise, you will create an additional MAC Address Pool in Virtual Machine Manager.
Mindset	While you have the two default MAC address pools that come with VMM, you can also create custom MAC address pools for virtual machines that are running on managed hosts. The static address pools can be used by VMM to automatically generate and assign MAC addresses to new virtual network devices.
Completion time	15 minutes

1. On Server01, in the VMM console, in the Fabric pane, under Networking, click **MAC Address Pools**.

Question 12	*What is the beginning MAC address used by Hyper-V clients?*

2. On the Home tab, in the Show group, click **Fabric Resources**. Then in the Create group, click **Create MAC Pool**.

3. In the Create MAC Address Pool Wizard, on the Name and Host Group page, in the MAC address pool name text box, type **MAC Address Pool 1**.

4. Under Host groups, select **All Hosts**. Click **Next**.

5. On the MAC Address Range page, specify the following:

   Starting MAC address: **06-3F-70-80-FF-A0**

   Ending MAC address: **06-3F-70-80-FF-AF**

Question 13	*How many addresses are available?*

6. Click **Next**.

7. On the Summary page, confirm the settings and then click **Finish**.

8. In the Jobs dialog box, make sure that the job has a status of Completed and then close the dialog box.

9. Take a screen shot of the MAC Pools pane by pressing **Alt+Prt Scr** and then paste it into your Lab 11 worksheet file in the page provided by pressing **Ctrl+V**.

Lab Challenge	Designing Virtualization Project III
Overview	You are an administrator for the Contoso Corporation, which produces smart devices for the home. Read Appendix A for background information about the company and then read the information presented in this exercise.
Mindset	Since you have been planning and designing your virtual environment, you are now ready to plan out the virtual networks for your organization. Therefore, you need to develop a plan for the Contoso Corporation that will create and configure IP address schemes, logical switches, logical networks, static IP pools, and VLANs.
Completion time	60 minutes

Modify the project plan that was started in Lab 9 and continued in Lab 10 by adding the planning and design of virtual networking. The proposal should include the following sections:

- Purpose of the Project
- Requirements of the Project
- The Proposed Solution

When writing the proposal, you must explain the reasoning behind your choices.

End of lab. You can log off or start a different lab. If you want to restart this lab, you'll need to click the End Lab button in order for the lab to be reset.

LAB 12
PLANNING AND IMPLEMENTING VIRTUALIZATION STORAGE

THIS LAB CONTAINS THE FOLLOWING EXERCISES AND ACTIVITIES:

BEFORE YOU BEGIN

The lab environment consists of student workstations connected to a local area network, along with a server that functions as the domain controller for a domain called contoso.com. The computers required for this lab are listed in Table 12-1.

Table 12-1
Computers required for Lab 12

Computer	***Operating System***	***Computer Name***
Server	Windows Server 2012 R2	RWDC01
Server	Windows Server 2012 R2	Server01
Server	Windows Server 2012 R2	Server03
Server	Windows Server 2012 R2	VServer01
Server	Windows Server 2012 R2	VServer02

In addition to the computers, you will also need the software listed in Table 12-2 to complete Lab 12.

Table 12-2
Software required for Lab 12

Software	***Location***
Lab 12 student worksheet	Lab12_worksheet.docx (provided by instructor)

Working with Lab Worksheets

Each lab in this manual requires that you answer questions, shoot screen shots, and perform other activities that you will document in a worksheet named for the lab, such as Lab12_worksheet.docx. You will find these worksheets on the book companion site. It is recommended that you use a USB flash drive to store your worksheets, so you can submit them to your instructor for review. As you perform the exercises in each lab, open the appropriate worksheet file, fill in the required information, and then save the file to your flash drive.

SCENARIO

After completing this lab, you will be able to:

- Plan and design virtual storage
- Create a VM using a file share

Estimated lab time: 90 minutes

Exercise 12.1	Planning Virtual Storage
Overview	In this written exercise, you will read the background information for the Contoso Corporation found in Appendix A. You will then read the information introduced in this lesson and answer the questions.
Mindset	When planning and configuring the Contoso virtual environment, you will need to plan the storage used by the virtual environment. As stated in Appendix A, you already have the SAN with iSCSI connections.
Completion time	20 minutes

Question 1	*How would you categorize the SAN (remote/local storage, block storage/file storage)?*

Question 2	*How would you classify the storage used by the SAN?*

Question 3	*You administer a remote site that does not have a SAN. You would like to create a failover cluster for high-available virtual machines at that site without installing a SAN. What can you do?*

Question 4	*At a remote site, a site server has several terabytes of free disk space. You have a powerful machine that you want to use to create a couple of test virtual machines. Besides making an iSCSI target out of the file server, what other option can you use to provide disk space to the power machine so that it can be used for virtual machines?*

Question 5	*You have to create a virtual environment for testing by users. You want to create 20 workstations that users will access to test applications. What can you do to use the least amount of disk space?*

Question 6	*Which steps should you use to connect the blades to the SAN so that you have high availability?*

Exercise 12.2	Creating a VM Using a File Share
Overview	In this exercise, you will create a virtual machine on a remote file share.
Mindset	You can also use a file server with SMB 3.0 to host storage, and the storage can be used with VMM. By adding a file server to VMM, VMM can automatically discover all the shares that are currently present on the server.
Completion time	25 minutes

1. On VServer01, log on using the **contoso\administrator** account and the **Pa$$w0rd** password.

2. Using Server Manager, open **Hyper-V Manager**.

3. Right-click **VServer01** and choose **Virtual Switch Manager**.

4. When the Virtual Switch Manager for VSERVER01 opens, click **Switch 1**.

5. Select the **Allow management operating system to share this network adapter** and then click **OK**.

6. Right-click the Network Status icon on the taskbar and choose **Open Network and Sharing Center**.

7. Click **vEthernet (Switch1)**.

8. In the VEthernet (Switch1) Status dialog box, click **Properties**.

9. In the VEthernet (Switch1) Properties dialog box, double-click **Internet Protocol Version 4 (TCP/IPv4)**.

10. Set the following and then click **OK**.

    IP address: **192.168.1.90**

    Subnet mask: **255.255.255.0**

    Preferred DNS server: **192.168.1.50**

11. Click **OK** to close the vEthernet (Switch1) Properties dialog box and then click **Close** to close the vEthernet (Switch1) Status dialog box.

12. Log out of VServer01.

13. On Server01, log on using the **contoso\administrator** account and the **Pa$$w0rd** password.

14. To open File Explorer, click the **File Explorer** icon on the task bar.
15. Double-click the **Local Disk (C:)** drive.
16. Create a folder called **VM**.
17. Right-click the **VM** folder and choose **Properties**.
18. In the VM Properties dialog box, click the **Sharing** tab and then click **Advanced Sharing**.
19. Select the **Share this folder** option and then click **Permissions**. In the Permissions for VM dialog box, select the **Allow Full Control** for Everyone. Click **OK**.
20. Click **OK** to close the Advanced Sharing dialog box.
21. Click **Close** to close the VM Properties dialog box.
22. Open the **VMM console** and click the **Fabric** workspace.
23. Under Servers, click **Cluster01**. Then right-click **Cluster01** and choose **Properties**.
24. On the Cluster01.contoso.com Properties dialog box, click the **File Share Storage** tab.
25. Click the **Add** button. In the Add File Share dialog box, in the File share path text box, type **\\server01.contoso.com\VM** and then click **OK**.
26. Click **OK** to close the Cluster01.contoso.com Properties dialog box.
27. Open the **VMs and Services** workspace.
28. Under All Hosts\Cluster01, right-click **vserver01** and choose **Properties**.
29. Click the **Hardware** tab.
30. Under Network Adapters, for the first Ethernet adapter, click **Logical network connectivity**.
31. In the Logical network connectivity pane, select the **192.168.1.0/24** subnet. When a warning appears, click **OK**. Click **OK** to close the vserver01.contoso.como Properties dialog box. If the 192.168.1.0/24 was already selected, deselect the **Network1** and **192.168.1.0/24** subnet option. Click **OK**. Then perform this step again.
32. Right-click **All Hosts** and choose **Create Virtual Machine**.
33. In the Create Virtual machine Wizard, on the Select Source page, select **Create the new virtual machine with a blank virtual hard disk** and then click **Next**.
34. On the Identity page, in the Virtual machine name text box, type **VM6** and then click **Next**.

35. On the Configure Hardware page, change the VM6_disk_1 disk to **5** GB.

36. Under Network Adapters, click the **Network Adapter 1**.

37. Select the **Connected to a VM network** option. Click **Next**.

38. On the Select Destination page, Place the virtual machines on a host option is selected and All Hosts is selected for the destination. Click **Next**.

39. On the Select Host page, select **vserver01.contoso.com** and then click **Next**.

40. On the Configure Settings page, in the Virtual machine path text box, ensure the path is **\\server01contoso.com\VM** and then click **Next**.

41. On the Add Properties page, click **Next**.

42. On the Summary page, click **Create**.

43. When the VM is created, close the Jobs dialog box.

44. Take a screen shot of the Virtual Machine Manager console by pressing **Alt+Prt Scr** and then paste it into your Lab 12 worksheet file in the page provided by pressing **Ctrl+V**.

Lab Challenge	Designing Virtualization IV
Overview	You are an administrator for the Contoso Corporation, which produces smart devices for the home. Read Appendix A for background information about the company and then read the information presented in this exercise.
Mindset	This phase of the plan includes planning and designing storage for the Contoso virtual environment.
Completion time	45 minutes

Modify the project plan that was started in Lab 9 and continued in Lab 10 and Lab 11 by adding the planning and design of virtual storage. The proposal should include the following sections:

- Purpose of the Project
- Requirements of the Project
- The Proposed Solution

When writing the proposal, you must explain the reasoning behind your choices.

End of lab. You can log off or start a different lab. If you want to restart this lab, you'll need to click the End Lab button in order for the lab to be reset.

LAB 13
PLANNING AND IMPLEMENTING VIRTUAL MACHINE MOVEMENT

THIS LAB CONTAINS THE FOLLOWING EXERCISES AND ACTIVITIES:

Exercise 13.1	Planning Virtual Machine Movement
Exercise 13.2	Perform a Live Migration
Lab Challenge	Designing Virtualization Project V

BEFORE YOU BEGIN

The lab environment consists of student workstations connected to a local area network, along with a server that functions as the domain controller for a domain called contoso.com. The computers required for this lab are listed in Table 13-1.

Table 13-1
Computers required for Lab 13

Computer	***Operating System***	***Computer Name***
Server	Windows Server 2012 R2	RWDC01
Server	Windows Server 2012 R2	Server01
Server	Windows Server 2012 R2	Server03
Server	Windows Server 2012 R2	VServer01
Server	Windows Server 2012 R2	VServer02

In addition to the computers, you will also need the software listed in Table 13-2 to complete Lab13.

Table 13-2
Software required for Lab 13

Software	***Location***
Lab 13 student worksheet	Lab13_worksheet.docx (provided by instructor)

Working with Lab Worksheets

Each lab in this manual requires that you answer questions, shoot screen shots, and perform other activities that you will document in a worksheet named for the lab, such as Lab13_worksheet.docx. You will find these worksheets on the book companion site. It is recommended that you use a USB flash drive to store your worksheets, so you can submit them to your instructor for review. As you perform the exercises in each lab, open the appropriate worksheet file, fill in the required information, and then save the file to your flash drive.

SCENARIO

After completing this lab, you will be able to:

- Plan and design live migration
- Perform a live and storage migration

Estimated lab time: 55 minutes

Exercise 13.1	Planning Virtual Machine Movement
Overview	In this written exercise, you will read the background information for the Contoso Corporation found in Appendix A. You will then read the information introduced in this lesson and answer the questions.
Mindset	Because of the ease with which VMs can be created and the speed at which they add services, VM management can quickly become a problem. When they become a challenge, you need a procedure whereby you can quickly move the VM and its storage with minimal inconvenience to your users.
Completion time	15 minutes

Question 1	*When using Virtual Machine Manager, which two types of VM migration are available?*

Question 2	*When using Virtual Machine Manager, what type of movement should be used to move a VM from one host to another host?*

Question 3	*You administer a LUN on a SAN that is running out of disk space. Therefore, you want to move one of the VMs to another LUN. Which type of migration should you perform?*

Question 4	*You administer a VMWare ESXi server running ESXi version 5.1, which has 8 VMs. You want to migrate these VMs to the Hyper-V environment. How would you perform the migration?*

Question 5	*You administer a physical server that you want to migrate as a virtual machine into your Hyper-V virtual environment. What would you do?*

Exercise 13.2	Perform a Live Migration
Overview	In this exercise, you will perform a live migration (LM) from one Hyper-V host to another Hyper-V host.
Mindset	LM is the process of moving a VM or its storage from one physical server to another physical server without turning off the VM and without any perceived or actual downtime. In prior versions of Windows Server, the process of performing LM required the VM to be hosted within a clustered environment
Completion time	15 minutes

1. On VServer02, log on using the **contoso\administrator** account and the **Pa$$w0rd** password.

2. Using Server Manager, open **Hyper-V Manager**.

3. Right-click **VServer02** and choose **Virtual Switch Manager**.

4. When the Virtual Switch Manager for VSERVER02 opens, click **Switch 1**.

5. Select the **Allow management operating system to share this network adapter** and then click **OK**.

6. Right-click the Network Status icon on the taskbar and choose **Open Network and Sharing Center**.

7. Click **vEthernet (Switch1)**.

8. In the VEthernet (Switch1) Status dialog box, click **Properties**.

9. In the VEthernet (Switch1) Properties dialog box, double-click **Internet Protocol Version 4 (TCP/IPv4)**.

10. Set the following and then click **OK**.

    IP address: **192.168.1.100**

    Subnet mask: **255.255.255.0**

    Preferred DNS server: **192.168.1.50**

11. Click **OK** to close the vEthernet (Switch1) Properties dialog box and then click **Close** to close the vEthernet (Switch1) Status dialog box.

12. Log out of VServer02.

13. On Server01, log on using the **contoso\administrator** account and the **Pa$$w0rd** password.

14. Open the VMM console and then click the **VMs and Services** workspace.

15. Under All Hosts, right-click **vserver02** and choose **Properties**.

16. Click the **Hardware** tab.

17. Under network adapters, click **Logical network connectivity**.

18. In the Logical network connectivity pane, select the **192.168.1.0/24** subnet. Click **OK** to close the vserver02.contoso.com.

19. Under the All Hosts node, right-click **vserver01** and choose choose **Properties**.

20. In the Properties dialog box, click the **Migration Settings** tab.

21. Under the Live migration settings section, make sure **Turn on incoming and outgoing live migration** is selected.

Question 6	*What is the maximum number of simultaneous live storage migrations allowed?*

Question 7	*Which authentication protocol is selected?*

22. Click **OK** to close the Properties dialog box.

23. Right-click **VM4** and choose **Migrate Virtual Machine**. If Migrate Virtual Machine is greyed out, right-click **VM4** and choose **Refresh**. Then try again.

24. In the Migrate VM Wizard, on the Select Host page, select **vserver02.contoso.com** and then click **Next**.

25. Take a screen shot of the Virtual Machine console showing the Summary page by pressing **Alt+Prt Scr** and then paste it into your Lab 13 worksheet file in the page provided by pressing **Ctrl+V**.

26. On the Summary page, click **Move**.

27. When the migration is complete, close the Jobs window.

28. Click Vserver02. Right-click **VM4** and choose **Migrate Storage**.

29. On the Select Path page, C:\ClusterStorage\Volume1 is already specified. Click **Next**.

30. On the Summary page, click **Move**.

31. When the migration is complete, close the Jobs window.

End of Exercise. Close all programs and windows.

Lab Challenge	Designing Virtualization Project V
Overview	You are an administrator for the Contoso Corporation, which produces smart devices for the home. Read Appendix A for background information about the company and then read the information presented in this exercise.
Mindset	This next phase of the plan involves planning and designing live migration for the Contoso virtual environment.
Completion time	40 minutes

Modify the project plan that was started in Lab 9 and continued in Lab 10, Lab 11, and Lab 12 by adding the planning and design of live migration. The proposal should include the following sections:

- Purpose of the Project
- Requirements of the Project
- The Proposed Solution

When writing the proposal, you must explain the reasoning behind your choices.

End of lab. You can log off or start a different lab. If you want to restart this lab, you'll need to click the End Lab button in order for the lab to be reset.

LAB 14
MANAGING AND MAINTAINING A SERVER VIRTUALIZATION INFRASTRUCTURE

THIS LAB CONTAINS THE FOLLOWING EXERCISES AND ACTIVITIES:

Exercise 14.1	Implementing VMM with Operations Manager
Exercise 14.2	Creating an Override for VMM PRO Management Packs
Exercise 14.3	Backing Up and Restoring a VM
Lab Challenge	Designing Virtualization Project VI

BEFORE YOU BEGIN

The lab environment consists of student workstations connected to a local area network, along with a server that functions as the domain controller for a domain called contoso.com. The computers required for this lab are listed in Table 14-1.

Table 14-1
Computers required for Lab 14

Computer	*Operating System*	*Computer Name*
Server	Windows Server 2012 R2	RWDC01
Server	Windows Server 2012 R2	Server01
Server	Windows Server 2012 R2	Server02
Server	Windows Server 2012 R2	Server03
Server	Windows Server 2012 R2	VServer01
Server	Windows Server 2012 R2	VServer02

In addition to the computers, you will also need the software listed in Table 14-2 to complete Lab 14.

Table 14-2
Software required for Lab 14

Software	*Location*
Lab 14 student worksheet	Lab14_worksheet.docx (provided by instructor)

Working with Lab Worksheets

Each lab in this manual requires that you answer questions, shoot screen shots, and perform other activities that you will document in a worksheet named for the lab, such as Lab14_worksheet.docx. You will find these worksheets on the book companion site. It is recommended that you use a USB flash drive to store your worksheets, so you can submit them to your instructor for review. As you perform the exercises in each lab, open the appropriate worksheet file, fill in the required information, and then save the file to your flash drive.

SCENARIO

After completing this lab, you will be able to:

- Plan and design a backup strategy for virtual machines
- Implement VMM with Operations Manager
- Create an override for VMM PRO Management Packs
- Using DPM, perform a backup and restore of a virtual machine

Estimated lab time: 135 minutes

Exercise 14.1	Implementing VMM with Operations Manager
Overview	In this exercise, you will integrate VMM with Operations Manager.
Mindset	To help monitor the health and availability of the virtual machines and virtual hosts that VMM manages, you can connect VMM with Operations Manager. You can also monitor the health and availability of the VMM management server, the VMM database server, and library servers.
Completion time	50 minutes

1. On Server01, log on using the **contoso\administrator** account and the **Pa$$w0rd** password.
2. To open File Explorer, click the **File Explorer** button on the taskbar. Open the **\\rwdc01\software** folder.
3. Double-click **ReportViewer**. If you are prompted to run the file, click **Run**.
4. In the Microsoft Report Viewer 2012 Runtime Wizard, on the Welcome page, click **Next**.
5. On the License Agreement page, click **I accept the terms in the license agreement** and then click **Next**.
6. On the Ready to Install the Program, click **Install**.
7. When the program is installed, click **Finish**.
8. Go back to the **\\rwdc01\software** folder.
9. Open the SC2012 R2 SCOM folder and then double-click the **Setup application**.
10. In the Operations Manager splash screen, click **Install**.
11. In the Operations Manager Setup Wizard, select the **Operations console** and then click **Next**.
12. On the Select installation location page, click **Next**.
13. On the Prerequisites page, click **Next**.
14. On the Please read the license terms page, select **I have read, understood, and agree with the license terms** and then click **Next**.
15. On the Help improve Operations Manager, select both **No, I am not willing to participate** options and then click **Next**.
16. On the Microsoft Update page, click **Off** and then click **Next**.

17. On the Installation Summary page, click **Install**.

18. When the installation is complete, click **Close**.

19. Open VMM Console and then click the **Settings** workspace.

20. In the main pane, click the **System Center Settings** node and then click the **Operations Manager Server**. Then right-click the **Operations Manager Server** and choose **Properties**.

21. In the Add Operations Manager Wizard, on the Introduction page, answer the following question and then click **Next**.

Question 1	*What are the required management packs in Operations Manager?*

22. On the Connection to Operations Manager page, in the Server name text box, type **server02.contoso.com** and then click **Next**.

23. On the Connection to VMM page, in the User name text box, type **contoso\administrator**. In the Password text box, type **Pa$$w0rd** and then click **Next**.

24. On the Summary page, click **Finish**.

25. After the New Operations manager connection job is complete, close the Jobs window.

26. Right-click **Operations Manager Server** and choose **Properties**.

27. Take a screen shot of the Operations Manager Settings Connection Details dialog box by pressing **Alt+Prt Scr** and then paste it into your Lab 14 worksheet file in the page provided by pressing **Ctrl+V**.

28. Click **OK** to close the Operations Manager Settings dialog box.

End of exercise. You can close all open programs.

Exercise 14.2	Creating an Override for VMM PRO Management Packs
Overview	In this exercise, you will open an Operations Manager monitor and create an override for a VMM PRO Management setting.
Mindset	Other settings can be configured by installing or customizing a System Center Operations Manager management pack. You customize the management pack by creating an override.
Completion time	15 minutes

1. On Server02, log on using the **contoso\administrator** account and the **Pa$$w0rd** password.

2. Open the **Operations Console** and then click the **Authoring** Workspace

3. Expand **Management Pack Objects** and then click **Monitors**.

4. Since Operations Manager can contain hundreds of management packs you should narrow the scope of the management pack objects. Therefore, at the top of the screen, click **Change Scope**.

5. Click the **View All targets** option and then click the **Clear All** button.

6. In the Look for text box, type **PRO**. Select all of the Management Packs that start with **Microsoft System Center Virtual Machine Manager** and then click **OK**.

7. In the Look for text box, type **CPU** and then click the **Find Now** button.

8. Click, then right-click **PRO CPU Utilization** and choose **Overrides > Override the Monitor > For all objects of another class...** Scroll down and select **PRO Hyper-V Host Target** and then click **OK**.

9. In the Override Properties dialog box, under the Parameter Name, select **Threshold** ,and then click its **Override** checkbox. Then for the Threshold value under Override Value, type **70**.

10. Take a screen shot of the Override Properties dialog box by pressing **Alt+Prt Scr** and then paste it into your Lab 14 worksheet file in the page provided by pressing **Ctrl+V**.

11. In the Select destination management pack section, click **New**.

12. In the Create a Management Pack Wizard, for the General Properties dialog box, in the Name text box, type **Contoso Management Pack**.

Question 2	*Which version is the management pack?*

13. Click **Next**.

14. For the Knowledge Article page, click **Create**.

15. Ensure the **Contoso Management Pack** is selected. Click **OK**.

End of exercise. You can close all open programs.

Exercise 14.3	Backing Up and Restoring a VM
Overview	In this exercise, you will use Data Protection Manager to back up and restore a virtual machine.
Mindset	DPM can protect virtual machines that are hosted on stand-alone servers or on clusters. DPM provides protection with online backups that do not affect the availability of the hosts or virtual machines. You can perform online backups with servers running Hyper-V based on Windows Server 2008, Windows Server 2008 R2, Windows Server 2012, or Windows Server 2012 R2. As with other backups, DPM can perform backups by using disk, tape, or cloud-based backups.
Completion Time	25 minutes

1. On Server01, log on using the **contoso\administrator** account and the **Pa$$w0rd** password.
2. Open Virtual Machine Manager.
3. Verify that VM4 is on vserver01. If it is not, on vserver02, right-click **VM4** and choose **Migrate Virtual Machine**. On the Select Host page, select **vserver01.contoso.com** and then click **Next**. On the Summary page, click **Move**. Close the Jobs window. Confirm that VM4 is now on vserver01.
4. On Server03, log on using the **contoso\administrator** account and the **Pa$$w0rd** password.
5. Open the **System Center 2012 R2 DPM Administrator Console** on the Desktop, and then click the **Protection** workspace.
6. On the ribbon, click **New**.
7. In the Create New Protection Group Wizard, on the welcome page, click **Next**.
8. On the Select Protection Group Type page, select **Servers** and then click **Next**.
9. On the Select Group Members page, under Available members, expand **Cluster01**, expand **SCVMM VM4 Resources**, and select **Hyper-V**. Click **Next**.
10. On the Select Data Protection Method page, in the Protection group name box, type **VM Protection Group**. Then make sure that the **I want short-term protection using Disk** option is selected. Click **Next**.
11. On the Specify Short-Term Goals page, accept the default settings and then click **Next**.
12. On the Review Disk Allocation page, click **Next**.
13. On the Choose Replica Creation Method page, click **Next**.

14. On the Consistency check options page, click **Next**.

15. On the Summary page, click **Create Group**.

16. Take a screen shot of the Create New Protection Group Status page by pressing **Alt+Prt Scr** and then paste it into your Lab 14 worksheet file in the page provided by pressing **Ctrl+V**.

17. Click **Close**.

18. If the status of the \Offline\VM4 is Replica creation in progress, wait until it is done. When the Status is OK, click **VM Protection Group**. Then right-click **\Offline\VM4** and choose **Create recovery point**.

19. In the Create recovery point dialog box, select **Create a recovery point by using express full backup** and then click **OK**.

20. When the recovery point has been created, take a screen shot of the Create Recovery Point dialog box by pressing **Alt+Prt Scr** and then paste it into your Lab 14 worksheet file in the page provided by pressing **Ctrl+V**.

21. Click **Close**.

22. Click the **Recovery** workspace.

23. Under Recoverable Data, click **contoso.com\SCVMM VM4 Resources (Cluster01)\All Protected HyperV Data\Offline\VM4**. With today's date selected, from the bottom pane, click the **Offline\VM4** and then, in the ribbon above, click **Recover**.

24. In the Recovery Wizard, on the Review Recovery Selection page, click **Next**.

25. On the Select Recovery Type page, answer the following question and then click **Next.**

Question 3	*Which option is selected?*

26. On the Specify destination page, click the **Browse** button. In the Specify Alternate Recovery Destination dialog box, expand **contoso.com\VSERVER01\Volumes\C:\\Cluster Storage\Volume 1** and then select **VM4**. Click **OK** to close the Specify Alternate Recovery Destination dialog box and then click **Next**.

27. On the Specify Recovery Options page, click **Next**.

28. On the Summary page, click **Recover**.

29. When the recovery has been completed successfully, take a screen shot of the Recovery Wizard by pressing **Alt+Prt Scr** and then paste it into your Lab 14 worksheet file in the page provided by pressing **Ctrl+V**.

End of exercise. You can close all open programs and log off from all servers.

Lab Challenge	Designing Virtualization Project VI
Overview	You are an administrator for the Contoso Corporation, which produces smart devices for the home. Read Appendix A for background information about the company and then read the information presented in this exercise.
Mindset	The planning and designing of the Contoso virtual environment is almost complete. The only thing that you need to add is how you are going to back up and restore the virtual environment.
Completion time	45 minutes

Modify the project plan that was started in Lab 9 and continued in Lab 10, Lab 11, and Lab 12 by adding the planning and design of a backup strategy. The proposal should include the following sections:

- Purpose of the Project
- Requirements of the Project
- The Proposed Solution

When writing the proposal, you must explain the reasoning behind your choices.

End of lab. You can log off or start a different lab. If you want to restart this lab, you'll need to click the End Lab button in order for the lab to be reset.

LAB 15
DESIGNING A CERTIFICATE SERVICES INFRASTRUCTURE

THIS LAB CONTAINS THE FOLLOWING EXERCISES AND ACTIVITIES:

Exercise 15.1	Planning a Certificate Infrastructure
Exercise 15.2	Installing a Root CA
Exercise 15.3	Installing a Subordinate CA
Lab Challenge	Designing a Certificate Services Infrastructure Project I

BEFORE YOU BEGIN

The lab environment consists of student workstations connected to a local area network, along with a server that functions as the domain controller for a domain called contoso.com. The computers required for this lab are listed in Table 15-1.

Table 15-1
Computers required for Lab 15

Computer	*Operating System*	*Computer Name*
Server	Windows Server 2012 R2	RWDC01
Server	Windows Server 2012 R2	Server01
Server	Windows Server 2012 R2	Server02

In addition to the computers, you will also need the software listed in Table 15-2 to complete Lab 15.

Table 15-2
Software required for Lab 15

Software	*Location*
Lab 15 student worksheet	Lab15_worksheet.docx (provided by instructor)

Working with Lab Worksheets

Each lab in this manual requires that you answer questions, shoot screen shots, and perform other activities that you will document in a worksheet named for the lab, such as Lab15_worksheet.docx. You will find these worksheets on the book companion site. It is recommended that you use a USB flash drive to store your worksheets, so you can submit them to your instructor for review. As you perform the exercises in each lab, open the appropriate worksheet file, fill in the required information, and then save the file to your flash drive.

SCENARIO

After completing this lab, you will be able to:

- Plan and design a certificate services infrastructure
- Install a root CA and a subordinate CA

Estimated lab time: 130 minutes

Exercise 15.1	Planning a Certificate Infrastructure
Overview	In this written exercise, you will read the background information for the Contoso Corporation found in Appendix A. You will then read the information introduced in this lesson and answer the questions.
Mindset	While some computers use digital certificates within the Contoso Corporation, the company has not had a PKI infrastructure. Therefore, you need determine the best way to deploy and implement a PKI.
Completion time	20 minutes

Question 1	*For the Contoso Corporation, you need to assign digital certificates to your client computers so that they can be used for VPN access and when encrypting documents. Which PKI implementation should you use (private, public or hybrid)?*

Question 2	*How many levels should the CA hierarchy have? What will the levels be used for?*

Question 3	*Would you recommend a standalone CA or an enterprise CA? Explain your answer.*

Question 4	*How can you ensure that the root CA is secure?*

Question 5	*Since your company has purchased Adatum, you would like the ability to assign certificates to Adatum's users and computers. You already have a VPN tunnel connecting the two organizations. How would you allow the deployment of Contoso certificates to Adatum users and computers?*

Question 6	*Which mechanism or mechanisms would you chose to validate certificates?*

Exercise 15.2	Installing a Root CA
Overview	In this exercise, you will install an enterprise root CA on Server01.
Mindset	The top of the certificate hierarchy is the root CA. Because everything branches from the root, it is trusted by all clients within an organization. Although smaller organizations have only one CA, larger organizations have a root CA with multiple subordinate CAs. Although the enterprise CA can issue certificates to end users, it is usually used to issue certificates to subordinate CAs.
Completion time	20 minutes

1. On Server01, log on using the **contoso\administrator** account and the **Pa$$w0rd** password.
2. In the Server Manager console, click **Manage** > **Add roles and features**.
3. In the Add Roles and Features Wizard, click **Next**.
4. On the Select installation type page, click **Next**.
5. On the Select destination server page, click **Next**.
6. On the Select server roles page, select **Active Directory Certificate Services**. In the Add Roles and Features Wizard window, click **Add Features** and then click **Next**.
7. On the Select features page, click **Next**.
8. On the AD CS page, click **Next**.
9. On the Select role services page, select **Certification Authority** and then click **Next**.
10. On the Confirm installation selections page, click **Install**.
11. On the Installation progress page, after installation is successful, click **Configure Active Directory Certificate Services on the destination server**.
12. On the Credentials page, click **Next**.
13. On the Select role services to configure page, click **Certification Authority** and then click **Next**.
14. On the Setup Type page, select **Enterprise CA.**

Question 7	*Which CA type does not require Active Directory?*

15. Click **Next**.

16. On the CA Type page, ensure that Root CA is selected and then click **Next**.

17. On the Private Key page, ensure that Create a new private key is selected and then click **Next**.

18. On the Cryptography for CA page, leave the default selections for Cryptographic Service Provider (CSP) and Hash Algorithm. For better security, change the Key length to **4096**.

Question 8	*Which hash algorithm is selected?*

19. Click **Next**.

20. On the CA Name page, answer the following question and then click **Next**.

Question 9	*What is the common name for this CA?*

21. On the Validity Period page, the default is 5 years. Click **Next**.

22. The CA Database page displays where the certificate database will be stored. Click **Next**.

23. On the Confirmation page, take a screen shot of the Confirmation page by pressing **Alt+Prt Scr** and then paste it into your Lab 15 worksheet file in the page provided by pressing **Ctrl+V**.

24. Click **Configure**.

25. On the Results page, click **Close**.

26. Click **Close** to close the Add Roles and Features Wizard.

Exercise 15.3	Installing a Subordinate CA
Overview	In this exercise, you will install an enterprise subordinate CA.
Mindset	Although there is only one root CA, there can be one or more subordinate CAs. The number of subordinate CAs needed is determined by geographical location and the number of clients.
Completion time	20 minutes

1. On Server02, log on using the **contoso\administrator** account and the **Pa$$w0rd** password.

2. In the Server Manager console, click **Manage** > **Add roles and features**.

3. In the Add Roles and Features Wizard, click **Next**.

4. On the Select installation type page, click **Next**.

5. On the Select destination server page, click **Next**.

6. On the Select server roles page, select **Active Directory Certificate Services**. In the Add Roles and Features Wizard window, click **Add Features** and then click **Next**.

7. On the Select features page, click **Next**.

8. On the Active Directory Certificate Services page, click **Next**.

9. On the Select role services page, select **Certification Authority** and then click **Next**.

10. On the Confirm installation selections page, click **Install**.

11. On the Installation progress page, after installation is successful, click **Configure Active Directory Certificate Services on the destination server**.

12. On the Credentials page, click **Next**.

13. On the Select role services to configure page, click **Certification Authority** and then click **Next**.

14. On the Setup Type page, select **Enterprise CA** and then click **Next**.

15. On the CA Type page, ensure that **Subordinate CA** is selected and then click **Next**.

16. On the Private Key page, ensure that **Create a new private key** is selected and then click **Next**.

17. On the Cryptography for CA page, leave the default selections for Cryptographic Service Provider (CSP) and Hash Algorithm. For better security, change the Key length to **4096** and then click **Next**.

18. On the CA Name page, click **Next**.

Question 10	*What is the Common name for this CA?*

19. On the Certificate Request page, select **Send a certificate request to a parent CA**. Then with the Parent CA setting, click **Select**, click **contoso-SERVER01-CA**, and then click **OK**. Click **Next**.

20. The CA Database page displays, where the certificate database will be stored. Click **Next**.

Question 11	*What is the location of the certificate database?*

21. On the Confirmation page, take a screen shot of the Confirmation page by pressing **Alt+Prt Scr** and then paste it into your Lab 15 worksheet file in the page provided by pressing **Ctrl+V**.

22. Click **Configure**.

23. On the Results page, click **Close**.

24. Click **Close** to close the Add Roles and Features Wizard.

Lab Challenge	Designing a Certificate Services Infrastructure Project I
Overview	You are an administrator for the Contoso Corporation, which produces smart devices for the home. Read Appendix A for background information about the company and then read the information presented in this exercise.
Mindset	You need to develop a plan to implement and deploy a PKI, which addresses how the organization will deploy digital certificates for your organization's users and computers.
Completion time	70 minutes

Create a proposal that includes the following sections:

- Purpose of the Project
- Requirements of the Project
- The Proposed Solution

When writing the proposal, you must explain the reasoning behind your choices.

End of lab. You can log off or start a different lab. If you want to restart this lab, you'll need to click the End Lab button in order for the lab to be reset.

LAB 16
IMPLEMENTING AND MANAGING A CERTIFICATE SERVICES INFRASTRUCTURE

THIS LAB CONTAINS THE FOLLOWING EXERCISES AND ACTIVITIES:

Exercise 16.1	Planning a Certificate Services Infrastructure
Exercise 16.2	Configuring a CRL
Exercise 16.3	Configuring an OCSP Responder
Exercise 16.4	Configuring the Certificate Enrollment Web Services and the Certificate Enrollment Policy Web Services
Lab Challenge	Designing a Certificate Services Infrastructure Project II

BEFORE YOU BEGIN

The lab environment consists of student workstations connected to a local area network, along with a server that functions as the domain controller for a domain called contoso.com. The computers required for this lab are listed in Table 16-1.

Table 16-1
Computers required for Lab 16

Computer	*Operating System*	*Computer Name*
Server	Windows Server 2012 R2	RWDC01
Server	Windows Server 2012 R2	Server01
Server	Windows Server 2012 R2	Server02

In addition to the computers, you will also need the software listed in Table 16-2 to complete Lab 16.

Table 16-2
Software required for Lab 16

Software	*Location*
Lab 16 student worksheet	Lab16_worksheet.docx (provided by instructor)

Working with Lab Worksheets

Each lab in this manual requires that you answer questions, shoot screen shots, and perform other activities that you will document in a worksheet named for the lab, such as Lab16_worksheet.docx. You will find these worksheets on the book companion site. It is recommended that you use a USB flash drive to store your worksheets, so you can submit them to your instructor for review. As you perform the exercises in each lab, open the appropriate worksheet file, fill in the required information, and then save the file to your flash drive.

SCENARIO

After completing this lab, you will be able to:

- Plan and design a certificate services infrastructure
- Configure a CRL
- Configure an OCSP Responder
- Configure the Certificate Enrollment Web Services and Certificate Enrollment Policy Web Services

Estimated lab time: 155 minutes

Exercise 16.1	Planning a Certificate Services Infrastructure
Overview	In this written exercise, you will read the background information for the Contoso Corporation found in Appendix A. You will then read the information introduced in this lesson and answer the questions.
Mindset	Since certificates is an important tool used in security, you need to plan your certificate services infrastructure so it will provide certificates easily, will be available when needed, and will be secure.
Completion time	20 minutes

Question 1	*When deploying several CAs, how can you deploy CAs with predefined values or parameters?*

Question 2	*The CA servers have the default validity period of 5 years. When should you renew the CA certificates?*

Question 3	*If you have an offline root, how can you renew the subordinate CA certificates?*

Question 4	*If you decide to use a stand-alone certificate authority, how can you configure the Active Directory users and computers to trust the certificate authority?*

Question 5	*You want to assign certificates for your routers and switches. What technology should you implement?*

Question 6	*For the Contoso Corporation, which CAs would you place the Certificate Enrollment Web Services?*

Question 7	*You need to allow the help desk to manage user certificates. Which role should you assign the help desk?*

Question 8	*Which tool should you use to monitor the CAs?*

Exercise 16.2	Configuring a CRL
Overview	In this exercise, you will configure a Certificate Revocation List (CRL) distribution point.
Mindset	Certificate Revocation List (CRL) is a digitally signed list issued by a CA that contains a list of certificates issued by the CA that have been revoked. The CDP extensions can be published to Active Directory, web servers (including FTP servers), and file servers. However, in order for your clients to be able to check the CRL, you have to specify those locations in the Certificate Authority console.
Completion time	15 minutes

1. On Server02, log on using the **contoso\administrator** account and the **Pa$$w0rd** password. When Server Manager opens, open the **Certification Authority** console.

2. In the Certification Authority console, expand the **contoso-SERVER02-CA** node. Then right-click **Revoked Certificates** and choose click **Properties**.

3. In the Revoked Certificates Properties window, set the CRL publication interval to **1 day** and the Delta CRL Publication interval to **1 hour** and then click **OK**.

4. Right-click the **contoso-SERVER02-CA** node and choose **Properties**.

5. Click the **Extensions** tab.

Question 9	*What is the http location for CRL distribution point?*

6. Click **http://<ServerDNSName>/CertEnroll/<CaName><CRLNameSuffix><DeltaCRLAllowed>.crl** and then click **Remove**. When you are prompted confirm that you want to remove the selected location, click **Yes**.

7. To add additional CRL points, click **Add**.

8. In the Add Location dialog box, in the Location text box, type **http://**. Then from the Variable option, select **<ServerDNSName>** and click **Insert**.

9. In the Location text box, type **/CertEnroll/**. Then from the Variable option, select **<CaName>** and click **Insert**.

10. Using the Variable option, add **<CRLNameSuffix><DeltaCRLAllowed>**.

11. In the Location text box, type **.crl**. When you are done, you should have:

    http://<ServerDNSName>/CertEnroll/<CaName><CRLNameSuffix><DeltaCRLAllowed>.crl

12. Take a screen shot of the Add Location text box by pressing **Alt+Prt Scr** and then paste it into your Lab 16 worksheet file in the page provided by pressing **Ctrl+V**.

13. Click **OK** to close the Add Location dialog box.

14. Click **OK** to close the Properties dialog box.

15. Click **Yes** to restart AC DS for the changes to take effect.

End of exercise. You can close the Certification Authority console.

Exercise 16.3	Configuring an OCSP Responder
Overview	In this exercise, you will configure an Online Certificate Status Protocol (OSCSP) responder.
Mindset	OCSP provides a system by which the HTTP protocol can be used to query the status of a digital certificate. Most OCSP responders get their data from published CRLs; other OCSP responders get their data from the CA's status database.
Completion time	35 minutes

1. On Server02, in the Server Manager console, click **Manage** > **Add roles and features**.

2. In the Add Roles and Features Wizard, click **Next**.

3. On the Select installation type page, click **Next**.

4. On the Select destination server page, click **Next**.

5. On the Select server roles page, expand **Active Directory Certificate Services** and select the following and click **Next**:

    - **Certificate Enrollment Policy Web Services**
    - **Certificate Enrollment Web Service**
    - **Certification Authority Web Enrollment**
    - **Network Device Enrollment Service**
    - **Online Responder**

    When you are asked to add features, click the **Add Features** button.

6. On the Select features page, click **Next**. On the Web Server Role (IIS) page, click **Next**. On the Select role services click **Next**.

7. On the Confirm installation selections page, click **Install**.

8. Click **Close** to close the Add Roles and Features Wizard.

9. Using Server Manager, click the yellow triangle with the black exclamation point and then click C**onfigure Active Directory Certificate Services on the destination server**.

10. In the AD CS Configuration wizard, on the Credentials page, click **Next**.

11. On the Role Services page, select **Online Responder** and then click **Next**.

12. Click **Configure**.

13. Click **Close**. When you are prompted to configure additional role services, click **No**.

14. Using Server Manager, open the **Certification Authority** console.

15. In the Certification Authority console, right-click the **contoso-SERVER02-CA** and choose **Properties**.

16. In the Properties dialog box, click the **Extensions** tab. For the Select extension, select **Authority Information Access (AIA)**.

Question 10	*What is the http location for Authority Information Access (AIA)?*

17. Click **Add**.

18. In the Add Location dialog box, in the Location text box, type **http://Server02/ocsp** and then click **OK**.

19. Click to select the **Include in the AIA extension of issued certificates** check box.

20. Click to select the **Include in the online certificate status protocol (OCSP) extension** check box and then click **OK**. If you are prompted to restart AD CS, click **Yes**.

21. On Server01, open a command prompt and execute the **certutil –crl** command. This will generate a c:\Windows\System32\CertSrv\CertEnroll\contoso-RWDC01-CA.crl.

22. Open **File Explorer** and navigate to **c:\Windows\System32\CertSrv\CertEnroll** folder. Then right-click the **contoso-RWDC01-CA** Certificate Revocation List file and choose **Copy**.

23. Using File Explorer, navigate to the **\\server01\c$\Windows\system32\certsrv\certenroll** folder. Then right-click the empty part of the window and choose **Paste**.

24. On Server02, go back to certificate authority. Right-click the **contoso-SERVER02-CA** node and choose **Stop Service**. Then right-click the **contoso-SERVER02-CA** node and choose **Start Service**. If the Certification Authority is not running, you have to start the service.

25. In the certsrv console, expand **contoso-SERVER02-CA** and then right-click the **Certificate Templates** folder and choose **Manage**.

26. In the Certificate Templates console, double-click the **OCSP Response Signing** template.

27. In the OCSP Response Signing Properties dialog box, click the **Security** tab. Under Permissions for Authenticated Users, select the **Allow** check box for **Enroll** and **Autoenroll**

28. Take a screen shot of the Security tab by pressing **Alt+Prt Scr** and then paste it into your Lab 16 worksheet file in the page provided by pressing **Ctrl+V**.

29. Click **OK**.

30. Close the Certificate Templates console.

31. In the Certification Authority console, right-click the **Certificate Templates** folder and choose **New > Certificate Template to Issue**.

32. In the Enable Certificate Templates dialog box, select the **OCSP Response Signing** template and then click **OK**.

33. Click the **Certificate Templates** node.

34. Take a screen shot of the certificate templates by pressing **Alt+Prt Scr** and then paste it into your Lab 16 worksheet file in the page provided by pressing **Ctrl+V**.

35. Using Server Manager, click **Tools** > **Online Responder Management**.

36. In the ocsp console, right-click **Revocation Configuration** and choose **Add Revocation Configuration**.

37. In the Add Revocation Configuration Wizard, click **Next**.

38. On the Name the Revocation Configuration page, in the Name text box, type **Contoso CA Online Responder** and then click **Next**.

39. On the Select CA Certificate Location page, the **Select a certificate for an Existing enterprise CA** option is already selected. Click **Next**.

40. On the Choose CA Certificate page, click **Browse**, click the certificate for **contoso-SERVER02-CA**, and then click **OK**. Click **Next**.

41. On the Select Signing Certificate page, verify that **Automatically select a signing certificate** is selected and **Auto-Enroll for an OCSP signing certificate** is selected and then click **Next**.

42. On the Revocation Provider page, click **Finish**.

43. Take a screen shot of the Online Responder Configuration by pressing **Alt+Prt Scr** and then paste it into your Lab 16 worksheet file in the page provided by pressing **Ctrl+V**.

44. Close the ocsp console.

Exercise 16.4	Configuring the Certificate Enrollment Web Services and the Certificate Enrollment Policy Web Services
Overview	In this exercise, you will configure the Certificate Web Enrollment Web Services and the Certificate Enrollment Policy Web Services.
Mindset	When you installed the Certificate Authority, you installed Certificate Enrollment Policy Web Services, Certificate Enrollment Web Services, and Certification Authority Web Enrollment on the subordinate CA. Before you can start using them, however, you also must configure these service roles.
Completion time	40 minutes

1. On RWDC01, log on using the **contoso\administrator** account and the **Pa$$w0rd** password.

2. On RWDC01, using Server Manager, open **Active Directory Users and Computers**.

3. In the Users OU, create a user account called **SVC-CERTS**. Configure the password as **Pa$$w0rd** and then configure the **password never to expire**.

4. Close **Active Directory Users and Computers**.

5. On Server02, using Server Manager, open **Computer Management**. Expand the **Local Users and Groups** and then click **Groups**.

6. Double-click **IIS_IUSRS**. In the IIS_IUSRS Properties dialog box, add the **contoso\SVC-CERTS** account and then click **OK**.

7. Close **Computer Management**.

8. On Server02, using Server Manager, click the yellow triangle with the black exclamation point and then click **Configure Active Directory Certificate Services on the destination server**.

9. In the AD CS Configuration wizard, on the Credentials page, click **Next**.

10. On the Role Services page, select the following options and then click **Next**.

    - **Certification Authority Web Enrollment**
    - **Certificate Enrollment Web Service**
    - **Certificate Enrollment Policy Web Service**

11. On the CA for CES page, click **Next**.

12. On the Authentication Type for CES page, the Windows integrated authentication option is already selected. Click **Next**.

13. On the Service Account for CES page, with Specify service account, click **Select**. When the Windows Security dialog box, login as **contoso\SVC-CERTS** with the password of **Pa$$w0rd**. Click **Next**.

14. On the Authentication Type for CEP page, Windows integrated authentication is already selected. Click **Next**.

15. On the Server Certificate page, select **Contoso-SERVER02-CA** and then click **Next**.

16. On the Confirmation page, take a screen shot of the AD CS Configuration by pressing **Alt+Prt Scr** and then paste it into your Lab 16 worksheet file in the page provided by pressing **Ctrl+V**.

17. Click **Configure**.

18. On the Results page, click **Close**.

19. If you are prompted to configure additional role services, click **No**.

20. Using Server Manager, click **Tools > Internet Information Services (IIS) Manager**.

21. Click **SERVER02**. Then under IIS, double-click **Server Certificates**.

22. In the Actions pane, click **Create Domain Certificate**.

23. When the Create Certificate wizard opens, on the Distinguished Name Properties, fill out the following and then click **Next**:

    Common name: **server02.contoso.com**

    Organization: **Contoso Corporation**

    Organization unit: **IT**

    City/locality: **Sacramento**

    State/province: **CA**

    Country/region: **US**

24. On the Online Certification Authority page, click **Select**.

25. On the Select Certification Authority, click **contoso-SERVER02-CA** and then click **OK**.

26. On the Online Certification Authority page, in the Friendly name text box, type **server02.contoso.com** and then click **Finish**.

27. In the Internet Information Services (IIS) Manager console, in the console tree, expand **SERVER02** node, the **Sites** node, and then click the **Default Web Site.**

28. In the Actions page, click **Bindings.**

29. In the Edit Site Binding dialog box opens, double-click https. For the SSL certificate, select **Server02.contoso.com**. Click **OK**.

30. Click **Close** to close the Site Bindings dialog box.

31. Right-click **Default Web Site** and choose **Manage Website** > **Restart**.

32. Click the **ADPolicyProvider_CEP_Kerberos** web service application. If you are prompted to stay connected with the latest Web Platform Components, click **No**.

33. In the ASP.NET section, double-click **Application Settings**.

34. Double-click **URI**.

Question 11	*What is the application string?*

35. Click **OK**.

36. On RWDC01, using Server Manager, click **Tools > Group Policy Management**.

37. In the Group Policy Management console, in the console tree, expand the **forest: contoso.com**, expand **Domains**, expand **contoso.com**, and click **Group Policy Objects**. Right-click the **Default Domain Policy** and choose **Edit**.

38. In the console tree under **Computer Configuration\Policies\Windows Settings\Security Settings**, click **Public Key Policies**.

39. Double-click **Certificate Services Client – Certificate Enrollment Policy**.

40. In the Certificate Services Client – Certificate Enrollment Policy dialog box, for the Configuration Model, select **Enabled**.

41. On the Confirmation page, take a screen shot of the Certificate Enrollment Policy Server dialog box by pressing **Alt+Prt Scr** and then paste it into your Lab 16 worksheet file in the page provided by pressing **Ctrl+V**.

42. Click **OK** to close the Certificate Services Client – Certificate Enrollment Policy dialog box.

End of exercise. You can close all programs and log off of all virtual machines.

Lab Challenge	Designing a Certificate Services Infrastructure Project II
Overview	You are an administrator for the Contoso Corporation, which produces smart devices for the home. Read Appendix A for background information about the company and then read the information presented in this exercise.
Mindset	While continuing to design and plan for the PKI, you need to determine how you are going to deploy digital certificates for your organization's users and computers.
Completion time	45 minutes

In this Lab Challenge, you will modify the project plan that you started in Lab 15 to explain how you will deploy and validate certificates. You should also explain how you are going to implement Administrator Role Separation. The proposal should include the following sections:

- Purpose of the Project
- Requirements of the Project
- The Proposed Solution

When writing the proposal, you must explain the reasoning behind your choices.

End of lab. You can log off or start a different lab. If you want to restart this lab, you'll need to click the End Lab button in order for the lab to be reset.

LAB 17 IMPLEMENTING AND MANAGING CERTIFICATES

THIS LAB CONTAINS THE FOLLOWING EXERCISES AND ACTIVITIES:

BEFORE YOU BEGIN

The lab environment consists of student workstations connected to a local area network, along with a server that functions as the domain controller for a domain called contoso.com. The computers required for this lab are listed in Table 17-1.

Table 17-1
Computers required for Lab 17

Computer	*Operating System*	*Computer Name*
Server	Windows Server 2012 R2	RWDC01
Server	Windows Server 2012 R2	Server01
Server	Windows Server 2012 R2	Server02
Server	Windows Server 2012 R2	Server03

In addition to the computers, you will also need the software listed in Table 17-2 to complete Lab 17.

Table 17-2
Software required for Lab 17

Software	*Location*
Lab 17 student worksheet	Lab17_worksheet.docx (provided by instructor)

Working with Lab Worksheets

Each lab in this manual requires that you answer questions, shoot screen shots, and perform other activities that you will document in a worksheet named for the lab, such as Lab17_worksheet.docx. You will find these worksheets on the book companion site. It is recommended that you use a USB flash drive to store your worksheets, so you can submit them to your instructor for review. As you perform the exercises in each lab, open the appropriate worksheet file, fill in the required information, and then save the file to your flash drive.

SCENARIO

After completing this lab, you will be able to:

- Create and deploy a certificate template
- Perform a manual enrollment of digital certificates
- Perform a CA web enrollment
- Configure autoenrollment of digital certificates
- Plan and design digital certificates

Estimated lab time: 115 minutes

Exercise 17.1	Creating and Deploying a Certificate Template
Overview	In this exercise, you will create a certificate template so that it can be used to deploy in future exercises.
Mindset	Certificate templates are used to simplify the task of administering a CA by allowing an administrator to identify, modify, and issue certificates that have been preconfigured for selected tasks. The Certificate Templates snap-in enables you to view and modify the properties for each certificate template and copy and modify certificate templates.
Completion time	20 minutes

1. On Server02, log on using the **contoso\administrator** account and the **Pa$$w0rd** password.
2. Using Server Manager, open the **Certification Authority** console.
3. Expand contoso-SERVER02-CA, right-click **Certificate Templates** and choose **Manage**.
4. In the Certificate Templates console, right-click the **User template** and choose **Duplicate Template**.
5. Click the **General** tab. In the template display name text box, type **CorporateUser**.

Question 1	*What is the validity period for the User certificate?*

6. Click the **Subject Name** tab.
7. Clear the **Include e-mail name in the subject** name check box and clear the **E-mail name** check box.
8. Click the **Extensions** tab.

Question 2	*What are the application policies for this template?*

9. Click **Application Policies** and then click **Edit**.
10. In the Edit Application Policies Extension dialog box, click **Add**.
11. In the Add Application Policy dialog box, click **Smart Card Logon**, and then click **OK** twice.
12. Click the **Superseded Templates** tab.

13. Click **Add**. Click the User template and then click **OK**.

14. Click **OK** to close the Properties of New Template dialog box.

15. Close the Certification Templates console.

16. In the Certification Authority console, right-click **Certificate Templates** and then choose **New > Certificate Template to Issue**.

17. In the Enable Certificate Templates window, select the **Corporate User** template and then click **OK**.

18. Take a screen shot of the Certification Authority console showing the Certificate Templates by pressing **Alt+Prt Scr** and then paste it into your Lab 17 worksheet file in the page provided by pressing **Ctrl+V**.

19. Close **Certification Authority**.

Exercise 17.2	Performing a Manual Enrollment
Overview	In this exercise, you will use the Certificates console to request a digital certificate.
Mindset	When you use manual enrollment, you create a private key and a certificate request is generated on a device such as a web service or a computer. The request is sent to the CA to generate the certificate. The certificate is sent back to the device for installation.
Completion time	20 minutes

1. On RWDC01, log on using the **contoso\administrator** account and the **Pa$$w0rd** password.

2. Using Server Manager, open **Active Directory Users and Computers**.

3. Open the **Users** OU, and double-click the **Administrator account**.

4. When the Administrator Properties dialog box opens, on the General tab, in the E-mail text box, type **administrator@contoso.com**.

5. To close the Administrator Properties dialog box, click **OK** and then close **Active Directory Users and Computers**.

6. On Server03, log on using the **contoso\administrator** account and the **Pa$$w0rd** password.

7. On Server03, right-click the **Start** button and choose **Run**. In the Run dialog box, in the Open text box, type **mmc** and then click **OK**.

8. In the console, click **File > Add/Remove snap-in**.

9. In the Add or Remove Snap-ins dialog box, double-click **Certificates**.

10. On the Certificates snap-in dialog box, click **My user account**. Click **Finish** and then click OK.

11. Expand the Certificates-Current User, expand and click **Personal**.

Question 3	*Why is the Personal\Certificates node not appearing?*

12. Right-click the Personal folder and choose **All Tasks > Request New Certificate**.

13. In the Certificate Enrollment wizard, click **Next**.

14. On the Certificate Enrollment Policy page, Active Directory Enrollment Policy is already selected. Click **Next**.

15. Click to select **CorporateUser** Certificate and then click **Enroll**.

16. After the certificate has been installed, click **Finish**.

17. Expand the **Personal** node and click the **Certificates** node.

18. Take a screen shot of the Certificates console showing the Personal Certificates by pressing **Alt+Prt Scr** and then paste it into your Lab 17 worksheet file in the page provided by pressing **Ctrl+V**.

End of exercise. You can leave the windows open for the following exercises.

Exercise 17.3	Performing a CA Web Enrollment
Overview	In this exercise, you will use the https://<servername>/certsrv website to request and install a digital certificate.
Mindset	The CA Web enrollment uses a website on a CA to obtain certificates. The website uses Internet Information Server (IIS) and the AD CS web enrollment service role. However, the AD CS web enrollment service role has to be configured before it is ready for use.
Completion time	10 minutes

1. On Server03, open Internet Explorer and type the following URL:

   https://Server02.contoso.com/certsrv

2. Login as **Contoso\administrator** with the password of **Pa$$w0rd** and then click **OK**.

3. Click **Request a certificate.**

4. On the Request a Certificate page, click **Advanced certificate request**.

5. On the Advanced Certificate Request, click **Create and submit a request to this CA**. If you are prompted to allow a website to perform digital certificate operation on your behalf, click **Yes**.

6. On the Advanced Certificate Request page, for the Certificate Template, select **CorporateUser**.

Question 4	*What is the key size?*

7. Click **Submit**. If you are prompted to allow a website to perform digital certificate operation on your behalf, click **Yes**.

8. On the Certificate issued page, click **Install this certificate**.

9. When the certificate has been installed, take a screen shot of Internet Explorer by pressing **Alt+Prt Scr** and then paste it into your Lab 17 worksheet file in the page provided by pressing **Ctrl+V**.

10. Close Internet Explorer.

Exercise 17.4	Performing Autoenrollment
Overview	In this exercise, you will enable autoenrollment for those certificates that allow autoenrollment based on permissions.
Mindset	Most certificates will be assigned through autoenrollment, which automatically deploys certificates to users, client computers, or servers. Autoenrollment can be applied only to enterprise CA (not standalone CA) and you have to deploy schema template version 2 or higher. In addition, the user needs Read, Enroll, and Autoenroll permissions for the certificate template to be deployed.
Completion time	20 minutes

1. On Server03, using the MMC/Certificate console, right-click the **Personal\Certificates** node and choose **Refresh**.

2. Right-click one of the **Administrator** certificates and choose **Delete**. When you are prompted to confirm that you want to delete the certificate, click **Yes**.

3. Delete the other **Administrator** certificate. Click **Yes** to continue.

4. On Server02, using the Certification Authority, right-click **Certificate Templates** and choose **Manage**.

5. Double-click the **CorporateUser** template. The Properties dialog box opens.

6. Click the **Security** tab.

Question 5	*Which permission is granted to domain users?*

7. Click **Domain Users** and then select **Allow Read, Allow Enroll** and **Allow Autoenroll**.

8. To close the CorporateUser Properties dialog box, click **OK**.

9. On RWDC01, using Server Manager, open **Group Policy Management**.

10. Expand **Forest: Contoso.**com and then expand **Domains**, expand **contoso.com,** and click **Group Policy Objects**. Right-click **Default Domain Policy** and choose **Edit**.

11. In the Group Policy Management Editor, expand **User Configuration**, expand **Policies**, expand **Windows Settings**, expand **Security Settings**, and then click to highlight **Public Key Policies**.

12. In the right pane, double-click **Certificate Services Client – Auto-Enrollment**.

13. In the Configuration Model drop-down list box, click **Enabled**.

14. Select the **Renew expired certificates, update pending certificates, and remove revoked certificates** option.

15. Select the **Update certificates that use certificate templates** option.

16. Click **OK** to close the Properties dialog box.

17. In the right pane, double-click the **Certificate Services Client – Certificate Enrollment Policy** object.

18. On the Enrollment Policy tab, set the Configuration Model to **Enabled** and then ensure that the certificate enrollment policy list displays the Active Directory Enrollment Policy.

19. Take a screen shot of Group Policy Management Editor by pressing **Alt+Prt Scr** and then paste it into your Lab 17 worksheet file in the page provided by pressing **Ctrl+V**.

20. Click **OK** to close the dialog box.

21. Close the Group Policy Management Editor and Group Policy Management console.

22. On Server03, right-click the **Start** button and choose **Command Prompt (Admin)**.

23. When the Command Prompt window opens, execute the following command:

    gpupdate /force

24. Wait a minute or two and right-click the **Certificates** node and choose **Refresh**.

25. Take a screen shot of **\Personal\Certificates** node showing the Administrator certificate by pressing **Alt+Prt Scr** and then paste it into your Lab 17 worksheet file in the page provided by pressing **Ctrl+V**.

End of Exercises. You can close all programs and log off from all servers.

Lab Challenge	Designing a Certificate Services Infrastructure Project III
Overview	You are an administrator for the Contoso Corporation, which produces smart devices for the home. Read Appendix A for background information about the company and then read the information presented in this exercise.
Mindset	While continuing the design and plan for the Contoso PKI, you need to determine which digital certificates to deploy and how those certificates will be deployed.
Completion time	45 minutes

In this Lab Challenge, you will modify the project plan that you started in Lab 15 to explain how you will deploy and validate certificates. In this Lab Challenge, you will modify the project plan that you started in Lab 15 to explain how you will deploy and validate certificates. You should also explain how you are going to implement Administrator Role Separation. The proposal should include the following sections:

- Purpose of the Project
- Requirements of the Project
- The Proposed Solution

When writing the proposal, you must explain the reasoning behind your choices.

End of lab. You can log off or start a different lab. If you want to restart this lab, you'll need to click the End Lab button in order for the lab to be reset.

LAB 18
DESIGNING AND IMPLEMENTING A FEDERATED IDENTITY SOLUTION

THIS LAB CONTAINS THE FOLLOWING EXERCISES AND ACTIVITIES:

Exercise 18.1	Planning Active Directory Federation Services
Exercise 18.2	Requesting and Importing Web Server Digital Certificates
Exercise 18.3	Implementing and Configuring AD FS
Exercise 18.4	Configuring Web Application Proxy
Lab Challenge	Designing an AD FS Solution

BEFORE YOU BEGIN

The lab environment consists of student workstations connected to a local area network, along with a server that functions as the domain controller for a domain called contoso.com. The computers required for this lab are listed in Table 18-1.

Table 18-1
Computers required for Lab 18

Computer	*Operating System*	*Computer Name*
Server	Windows Server 2012 R2	RWDC01
Server	Windows Server 2012 R2	Server01
Server	Windows Server 2012 R2	Server02
Server	Windows Server 2012 R2	Server03
Server	Windows Server 2012 R2	VServer01

In addition to the computers, you will also need the software listed in Table 18-2 to complete Lab 18.

Table 18-2
Software required for Lab 18

Software	*Location*
Lab 18 student worksheet	Lab18_worksheet.docx (provided by instructor)

Working with Lab Worksheets

Each lab in this manual requires that you answer questions, shoot screen shots, and perform other activities that you will document in a worksheet named for the lab, such as Lab18_worksheet.docx. You will find these worksheets on the book companion site. It is recommended that you use a USB flash drive to store your worksheets, so you can submit them to your instructor for review. As you perform the exercises in each lab, open the appropriate worksheet file, fill in the required information, and then save the file to your flash drive.

SCENARIO

After completing this lab, you will be able to:

- Plan and design Active Directory Federation Services
- Request and import web server digital certificates
- Implement and configure Active Directory Federation Services
- Configure Web Application Proxy

Estimated lab time: 150 minutes

Exercise 18.1	Planning Active Directory Federation Services
Overview	In this written exercise, you will read the background information for the Contoso Corporation found in Appendix A. You will then read the information introduced in this lesson and answer the questions.
Mindset	Thus far, the Contoso Corporation has used basic web applications. However, the developers are looking at developing several claims-aware applications. Some of these applications will only be used by employees, while other applications will be used by external customers.
Completion time	20 minutes

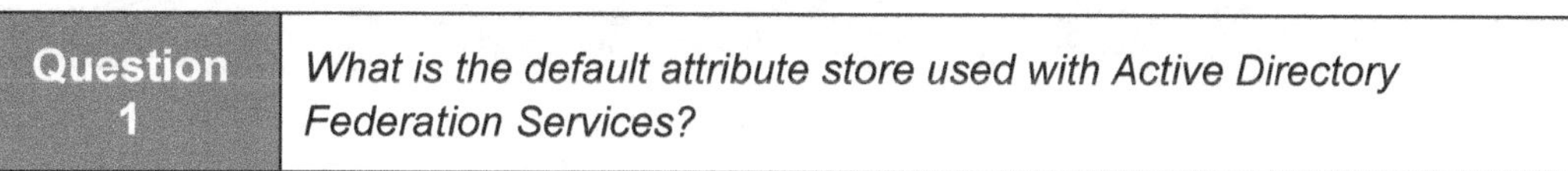

Question 1	*What is the default attribute store used with Active Directory Federation Services?*

Question 2	*Which AD FS deployment goal should be used when you have your user's access internal applications and services via AD FS?*

Question 3	*How many digital certificates will you need to acquire to use AD FS?*

Question 4	*Adatum Incorporated is a company that you have purchased but runs its own forest, domain, and certificate authority. You want Adatum users to access a new HR application using AD FS. Which certificates would you need and how would you configure them?*

Question 5	*In AD FS, which technology allows you to use certificates and username/passwords for authentication?*

Question 6	*Contoso wants to build a claims-aware application for external customers. Since these customers will not have Active Directory accounts, what should you use to keep track of your users?*

Question 7	*What should you use to help protect and separate your AD FS for users that access the claims-aware applications over the Internet?*

Exercise 18.2	Requesting and Importing Web Server Digital Certificates
Overview	In this exercise, you will use a copy of the Web Server certificate template to create a certificate template so the certificate with private keys can be exported. Different from previous courses, you will not be guided through each step. Instead, you must determine the best way to deploy the application based on the guidelines provided. You will then perform a request on Vserver01 for vserver01.contoso.com and install the certificate on VServer01 and VServer02.
Mindset	To perform AD FS and Application Web Proxy, you will need to request and install a certificate on the AD FS server. When the certificate is installed, you will have to export the certificate and then install the certificate to VServer02.
Completion time	30 minutes

When done, take a screen shot of the Certification Authority showing the certificate templates by pressing **Alt+Prt Scr** and then paste it into your Lab 18 worksheet file in the page provided by pressing **Ctrl+V**.

Exercise 18.3	Implementing and Configuring AD FS
Overview	In this exercise, you will deploy Active Directory Federation Services to VServer01 including installing the Active Directory Federation Services role and creating a standalone Federation Server. Unlike previous courses, you will not be guided through each step. Instead, you must determine the best way to deploy the application based on the guidelines provided.
Mindset	AD FS role allows administrators to configure Single Sign-On (SSO) for web-based applications across a single organization or multiple organizations without requiring users to remember multiple usernames and passwords. It is also a requirement for Web Application Proxy.
Completion time	20 minutes

When AD FS is configured, take a screen shot of the Remote Access Management Console Remote Access Review window by pressing **Alt+Prt Scr** and then paste it into your Lab 18 worksheet file in the page provided by pressing **Ctrl+V**.

Exercise 18.4	Configuring Web Application Proxy
Overview	In this exercise, on VServer02, you will deploy a Web Application Proxy so that it can be used to publish external applications.
Mindset	A reverse proxy is a proxy server that retrieves resources from servers on behalf of a client. The resources are then relayed through the proxy server to the client. As far as the client is concerned, the resources originate from the server itself. The Web Application Proxy can be used to hide the existence of the resource server and has the ability to selectively access the necessary applications on the servers inside the organization from the outside. Therefore, by using a reverse proxy, you protect applications from external threats and help protect internal resources by providing a Defense in Depth approach.
Completion time	20 minutes

When the Web Application Proxy Configuration Wizard is configured successfully, take a screen shot of the Remote Access Management Console Remote Access Review window by pressing **Alt+Prt Scr** and then paste it into your Lab 18 worksheet file in the page provided by pressing **Ctrl+V**.

Lab Challenge	Designing an AD FS Solution
Overview	You are an administrator for the Contoso Corporation, which produces smart devices for the home. Read Appendix A for background information about the company and then read the information presented in this exercise.
Mindset	You have been assigned to work with the developer team and network team to install and configure several claims-aware applications. Some of the applications are HR applications that will be used by internal employees. Other applications are customer applications that will allow users to access support status of their orders and purchased products. You need to develop a plan to deploy these applications.
Completion time	60 minutes

Create a proposal that includes the following sections:

- Purpose of the Project
- Requirements of the Project
- The Proposed Solution

When writing the proposal, you must explain the reasoning behind your choices.

End of lab. You can log off or start a different lab. If you want to restart this lab, you'll need to click the End Lab button in order for the lab to be reset.

LAB 19
DESIGNING AND IMPLEMENTING ACTIVE DIRECTORY RIGHTS MANAGEMENT SERVICES

THIS LAB CONTAINS THE FOLLOWING EXERCISES AND ACTIVITIES:

Exercise 19.1	Planning AD RMS
Exercise 19.2	Configuring AD RMS Prerequisites
Exercise 19.3	Installing AD RMS
Exercise 19.4	Managing Trusted User Domains
Lab Challenge	Designing an AD RMS

BEFORE YOU BEGIN

The lab environment consists of student workstations connected to a local area network, along with a server that functions as the domain controller for a domain called contoso.com. The computers required for this lab are listed in Table 19-1.

Table 19-1
Computers required for Lab 19

Computer	***Operating System***	***Computer Name***
Server	Windows Server 2012 R2	RWDC01
Server	Windows Server 2012 R2	Server02
Server	Windows Server 2012 R2	Server03

In addition to the computers, you will also need the software listed in Table 19-2 to complete Lab 19.

Table 19-2
Software required for Lab 19

Software	***Location***
Lab 19 student worksheet	Lab19_worksheet.docx (provided by instructor)

Working with Lab Worksheets

Each lab in this manual requires that you answer questions, shoot screen shots, and perform other activities that you will document in a worksheet named for the lab, such as Lab19_worksheet.docx. You will find these worksheets on the book companion site. It is recommended that you use a USB flash drive to store your worksheets, so you can submit them to your instructor for review. As you perform the exercises in each lab, open the appropriate worksheet file, fill in the required information, and then save the file to your flash drive.

SCENARIO

After completing this lab, you will be able to:

- Plan and design AD RMS
- Install and configure AD RMS
- Manage Trusted User Domains

Estimated lab time: 115 minutes

Exercise 19.1	Planning **AD RMS**
Overview	In this written exercise, you will read the background information for the Contoso Corporation found in Appendix A. You will then read the information introduced in this lesson and answer the questions.
Mindset	You are assessing how to provide an extra level of security by encrypting confidential files. Your manager has decided to implement Active Directory Rights Management Services.
Completion time	15 minutes

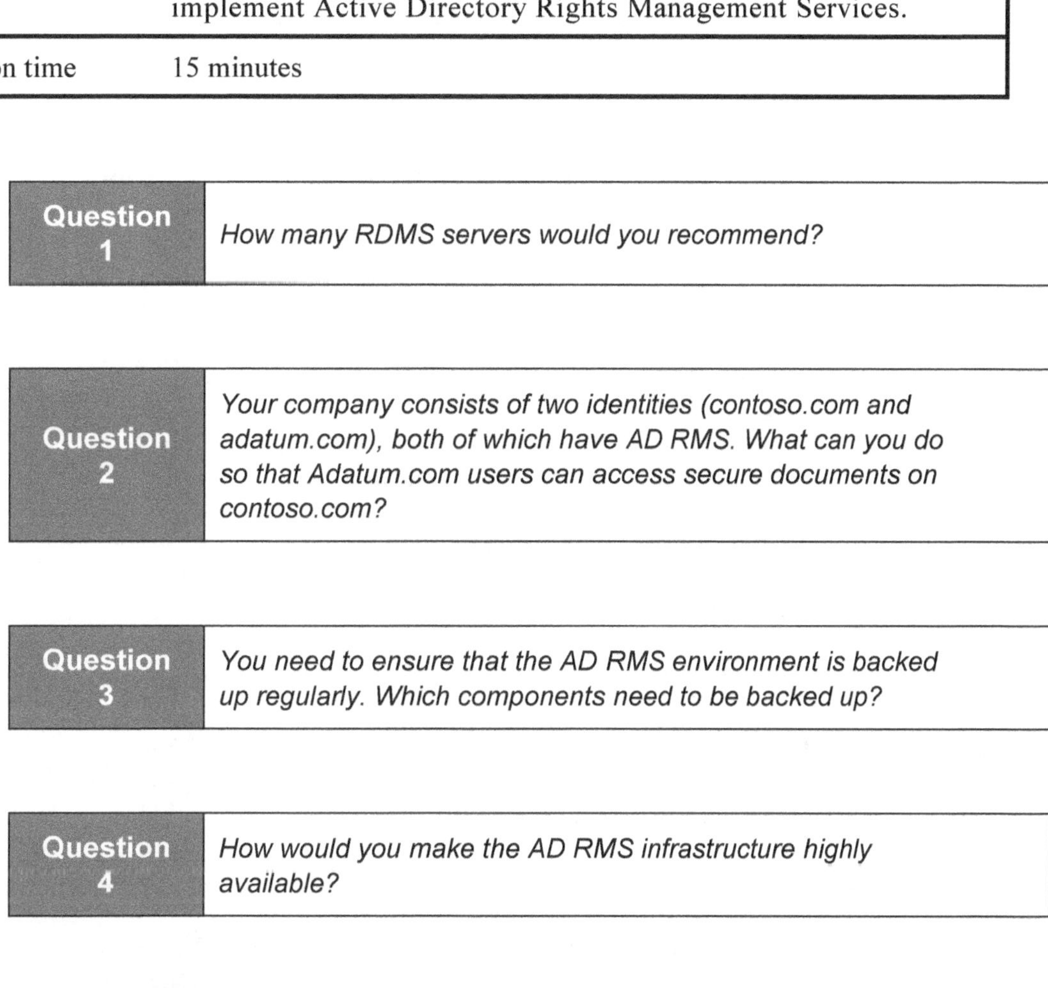

Question 1	*How many RDMS servers would you recommend?*

Question 2	*Your company consists of two identities (contoso.com and adatum.com), both of which have AD RMS. What can you do so that Adatum.com users can access secure documents on contoso.com?*

Question 3	*You need to ensure that the AD RMS environment is backed up regularly. Which components need to be backed up?*

Question 4	*How would you make the AD RMS infrastructure highly available?*

Question 5	*At Contoso, which systems can make use of the AD RMS system?*

Exercise 19.2	Configuring AD RMS Prerequisites
Overview	In this exercise, you will prepare the servers so that you can install and configure AD RMS.
Mindset	User accounts must have email addresses assigned in Active Directory. In addition, you will need a service account and you will need to configure DNS.
Completion time	20 minutes

1. On RWDC01, log on using the **contoso\administrator** account and the **Pa$$w0rd** password.

2. On a domain controller, using Server Manager, click T**ools** > **Active Directory Administrative Center**.

3. On the Active Directory Administrative Center, right-click **Contoso (local)** and choose **New** > **Organizational Unit**.

4. In the Create Organizational Unit dialog box, type **Service Accounts** in the Name text box and then click **OK**.

5. Right-click the **Service Accounts** OU and choose **New** > **User**.

6. In the Create User dialog box, type the following:

   First name: **ADRMS_SVC**

   User UPN logon: **ADRMS_SVC**

   Password: **Pa$$w0rd**

   Password options: **Other password options**

   Password never expires: **Enabled**

   User cannot change password: **Enabled**

7. Take a screen shot of the Active Directory Administrative Center console by pressing **Alt+Prt Scr** and then paste it into your Lab 19 worksheet file in the page provided by pressing **Ctrl+V**.

8. Create an additional user named John Smith (as in Step 6) and use John.Smith as the User UPN logon.

9. Click **OK** to close the Create User dialog box.

10. Right-click **Users** organization unit and choose **New** > **Group**.

11. In the New Object - Group dialog box, in the Group name text box, type **RMS Users**.

12. Click **Members**.

13. Click **Add**. Type **John Smith** and then click **OK**.

14. Click **OK** to close the Create Group dialog box.

15. Click **contoso (local)** and click **Users**.

16. Double-click **John Smith**.

Question 6	*When assigning access to AD RMS and protected documents, what is used to identify users?*

17. In the John Smith dialog box, in the E-mail text box, type **John.Smith@contoso.com**. Click **OK**.

18. Close Active Directory Administrative Center.

19. Using Server Manager, click **Tools** > **DNS**.

20. In DNS Manager, expand **RWDC01**, expand **Forward Lookup Zones**, and then click **contoso.com**.

21. Right-click the **contoso.com** domain and choose **New Alias (CNAME)**.

22. In the New Resource Record dialog box, type the following:

    Alias name: **ADRMS**

    Fully qualified domain name (FQDN) for target host: **server02.contoso.com**

23. Click **OK** to close the New Resource Record dialog box.

24. Close DNS Manager.

Exercise 19.3	Installing **AD RMS**
Overview	In this exercise, you will install and configure AD RMS on Server02.
Mindset	An AD RMS deployment consists of one or more servers known as a cluster. Additional servers can be added for scalability (if you use a dedicated SQL server). When you deploy AD RMS in a single forest, it's considered a single AD RMS cluster.
Completion time	20 minutes

1. On Server02, log on using the **contoso\administrator** account and the **Pa$$w0rd** password.
2. Using Server Manager, click **Manage** > **Add Roles and Features**.
3. In the Add Roles and Features Wizard, click **Next**.
4. On the Select installation type page, click **Next**.
5. On the Select destination server page, click **Next**.
6. Click to select **Active Directory Rights Management Services**. When you are prompted to add features, click **Add Features**.
7. Back on the Select server roles page, click **Next**.
8. On the Select features page, click **Next**.
9. On the Active Directory Rights Management Services page, click **Next**.
10. In the Role Services page, if Active Directory Rights Management Server is already selected, click **Next**. On the Web Server (IIS) page, click **Next**, and then on Role Services page, click **Next**.
11. On the Confirm installation selections page, click **Install**.
12. When the installation is complete, click **Close**.
13. Using Server Manager, click the **AD RMS** node.
14. At the top of the Servers section, next to Configuration required for Active Directory Rights Management Services at SERVER02, click **More**.
15. In the All Servers Task Details dialog box, click **Perform additional configuration**.
16. In the AD RMS Configuration wizard, on the AD RMS page, click **Next**.
17. On the AD RMS Cluster page, Create a new AD RMS root cluster is already selected. Click **Next**.

18. On the Configuration Database Server page, in the Server text box, click the **Select** button. In the Select Computer dialog box, in the Enter the object name to select text box, type **server03** and then click **OK**. In the Database Instance section, click **List**. Select **DefaultInstance** and then click **Next**.

19. On the Server Account page, click **Specify**.

20. In the Windows Security dialog box, type the following details, click **OK**, and then click **Next**:

    - Username: **ADRMS_SVC**
    - Password: **Pa$$w0rd**

21. On the Cryptographic Mode page, click **Cryptographic Mode 2**. Answer the following question and then click **Next**.

Question 7	*What does Cryptographic Mode 2 consist of?*

22. On the Cluster Key Storage page, click **Use AD RMS centrally managed key storage** and then click **Next**.

23. On the Cluster Key Password page, in the Password text box and the Confirm Password text box, type **Pa$$w0rd** and then click **Next**.

24. On the Cluster Web Site page, verify that Default Web Site is selected and then click **Next**.

25. On the Cluster Address page, provide the following information and then click Next:

    - Connection Type: **Use an unencrypted connection (http://)**
    - Fully Qualified Domain Name: **adrms.contoso.com**
    - Port: **80**

26. On the Licensor Certificate page, type **Contoso AD RMS** and then click **Next**.

27. On the SCP Registration page, click **Register the SCP now** and then click **Next**.

28. On the Confirmation page, click **Install**.

29. When the installation is successful, take a screen shot of the Results page by pressing **Alt+Prt Scr** and then paste it into your Lab 19 worksheet file in the page provided by pressing **Ctrl+V**.

30. Click **Close**.

31. To manage AD RMS, you must sign out of Windows. Therefore, click **Start > Administrator** and then click **Sign Out**.

Exercise 19.4	Managing Trusted User Domains
Overview	In this exercise, you will export the Trusted User Domains (TUDs) and then import them.
Mindset	By default, AD RMS does not service requests from users whose rights account certificate (RAC) was issued by a different AD RMS server. However, you can add user domains to the list of TUDs, which allows AD RMS to process the requests.
Completion time	10 minutes

1. On Server02, log on using the **contoso\administrator** account and the **Pa$$w0rd** password.

2. Using Server Manager, click **Tools** > **Active Directory Rights Management Services**.

3. In the Active Directory Rights Management Services console, expand **Trust Policies** and then click **Trusted User Domains**.

4. In the Center pane, under the Trusted User Domain Information section, right-click the **Enterprise** certificate and choose **Export Trusted User Domain**.

Question 8	*What is the name and type of the Trusted User Domain?*

5. In the Export Trusted User Domain As dialog box, in the File name text box, type **\\rwdc01\software\EnterpriseTUD** and then click **Save**.

6. In the Actions pane, click **Import Trusted User Domain**.

7. In the Trusted user domain file text box, click Browse, click **\\rwdc01\software\EnterpriseTUD.bin**, and then click **Open**.

8. In the Display name text box, type **Enterprise**.

9. Take a screen shot of the Import trusted user domain file page by pressing **Alt+Prt Scr** and then paste it into your Lab 19 worksheet file in the page provided by pressing **Ctrl+V**.

10. Click **Finish**.

11. Since the TUD certificate is already installed, you a dialog box will appear, indicating that it is already imported and trusted. Click **OK** and then click **Cancel**.

Lab Challenge	Designing an **AD RMS**
Overview	You are an administrator for the Contoso Corporation, which produces smart devices for the home. Read Appendix A for background information about the company and then read the information presented in this exercise.
Mindset	As specified by your manager, you need to develop a plan to install and configure Active Directory Rights Management so that you can protect confidential documents. In addition, the plan should include how you will roll out the use of Active Directory Rights Management.
Completion time	60 minutes

Create a proposal that includes the following sections:

- Purpose of the Project
- Requirements of the Project
- The Proposed Solution

When writing the proposal, you must explain the reasoning behind your choices.

End of lab. You can log off or start a different lab. If you want to restart this lab, you'll need to click the End Lab button in order for the lab to be reset.

APPENDIX A CONTOSO CORPORATION OVERVIEW

The Contoso Corporation is a leading company in producing smart devices for the home, including smart doors, smart vacuums, smart lamps, smart heating and cooling systems, smart windows, smart shades, smart clocks, smart exercise equipment, smart dish washers, smart refrigerators, smart televisions, smart radios, smart beds, smart chairs, and smart sinks. The Contoso Corporation began as a security system consultant company consisting of five employees and has grown to an international company with 8,000 employees.

PHYSICAL SITES

The Corporate office is in Sacramento, California, with a campus consisting of three buildings:

- Building Sacramento-A: Offices for 400 employees. Sacramento-A hosts a large number of executives, including the president, most of the vice presidents, the chief financial officer, and the chief information officer. It also includes the corporate marketing team, the corporate accounting team, and the corporate legal team. The main information technology group is located in Sacramento-A, which also hosts the company's largest data center.
- Building Sacramento-B: Offices for 320 employees. Sacramento-B hosts the corporate design and testing teams.
- Building Sacramento-C: Offices for 420 employees. Sacramento-C hosts the marketing team, the corporate sales team, and miscellaneous staff positions.

The Contoso Corporation has grown quickly by purchasing other companies in an effort to acquire patents, designs, and technical staff for various products and technology. As a result, the Contoso Corporation has 8 manufacturing sites, each with 300-500 employees. Each manufacturing site consists of a server room. The manufacturing sites are situated in the following locations:

- Detroit
- Miami
- Dallas
- Pittsburgh
- Phoenix
- Seattle
- Oklahoma City
- Portland

The call center, which handles customer questions and problems, is located in Cleveland. The call center is open 24/7. 380-560 employees are located there, depending on the call volume and season. There are four distribution centers in Reno, Austin, Albany, and Denver. Each site has 300 to 400 employees.

The majority of the other employees are sales personnel and in-house consultants who create customized solutions for home owners throughout the United States. They reside in 78 sites, each consisting of 10-25 employees.

Recently, the Contoso Corporation has purchased Adatum Incorporated, which is located in Chicago. Adatum Incorporated employs 130 employees. However, since some of the positions will be redundant, you should expect that approximately 30 users will not be retained.

ACTIVE DIRECTORY

The Contoso Corporation uses two forests. The primary forest/domain is contoso.com. There is also a subdomain called support.contoso.com.

In the Contoso.com domain, you have the following organizational units:

- Executives
- Marketing
- Accounting
- Legal
- Design
- Testing
- Information Technology
- Sales
- Distribution

In the support.contoso.com domain, you have the following organizational units:

- Managers
- Call Personnel

The forest/domain for Adatum Incorporated is adatum.com. While Adatum Incorporated has its own IT team, you will be taking over their resources and eventually merging Adatum's resources into the contoso.com forest.

The Contoso.com domain has the following domain controllers:

- RWDC01 (Windows Server 2012 R2) – Sacramento – GC and DNS*
- RWDC02 (Windows Server 2012 R2) – Sacramento – PDC Emulator, Infrastructure Master, RID Master, Schema Master, Domain Naming Master, and DNS*
- RWDC03(Windows Server 2012) – Detroit – DNS
- RWDC04 (Windows Server 2008 R2) – Miami – GC and DNS
- RWDC05 (Windows Server 2008 R2) – Dallas – GC and DNS

- RWDC06 (Windows Server 2008 R2) – Pittsburgh – DNS
- RWDC07 (Windows Server 2008 R2) – Phoenix – GC and DNS
- RWDC08 (Windows Server 2008 R2) – Seattle – DNS
- RWDC09 (Windows Server 2008 R2) – Oklahoma City – GC and DNS
- RWDC10 (Windows Server 2008 R2) – Portland – GC and DNS

* A virtual server running on Windows Server 2012 R2 Hyper-V

The support.contoso.com domain has the following domain controllers:

- RWDC11 (Windows Server 2008 R2) – GC, PDC Emulator, Infrastructure Master, RID Master, and DNS

The Adatum.com forest/domain has two domain controllers:

- ARWDC01 (Windows Server 2008 R2) – GC and DNS
- ARWDC02 (Windows Server 2008 R2) – GC, PDC Emulator, Infrastructure Master, RID Master, Schema Master, Domain Naming Master, and DNS

SERVERS

Because Contoso is a large company with many products and designs, there are many servers throughout the various sites. As a new administrator at Contoso, you will need to evaluate file storage and access so files are accessible to users yet also secure. Each site (except the corporate office and call center) will have 2-4 file servers/print servers.

Within the data center, there are two chassis; each chassis has four blades running Windows Server 2012 R2 Datacenter and Hyper-V. The blades are connected to a SAN using iSCSI connections. In addition, the corporate office has the following servers:

- 4 mail servers running Microsoft Windows Server 2012 R2 and Microsoft Exchange 2013
- 4 database servers running Microsoft Windows Server 2012 R2 and Microsoft SQL 2012
- 4 content management servers running Microsoft Windows Server 2008 R2 and Microsoft SharePoint 2010 servers*
- 12 application servers running Windows Server 2008 R2, Windows Server 2012 and Windows Server 2012 R2*
- 8 internal web servers running Windows Server 2008 R2, Windows Server 2012, and Windows Server 2012 R2*
- 8 external web servers (placed in the DMZ) running Windows Server 2008 R2*
- 2 external DNS servers (placed in the DMZ) running Windows Server 2008 R2
- 2 internal DHCP servers in a failover cluster running Windows Server 2008 R2
- 5 file servers running Windows Server 2008 R2, Windows Server 2012, and Windows Server 2012 R2
- 5 file servers running Windows Server 2008 R2, Windows Server 2012, and Windows Server 2012 R2*.
- 2 print servers running Windows Server 2008 R2*

* A virtual server running on Windows Server 2012 R2 Hyper-V

The call center has the following servers:

- 4 file/print servers running Windows Server 2008 R2
- 4 application servers running Windows Server 2008 R2
- 4 internal web servers running Windows Server 2008 R2
- 2 servers running Windows Server 2008 R2 and Microsoft SQL Server 2010
- 1 DHCP server running Windows Server 2008 R2

Adatum has the following virtual servers running on Hyper-V:

- 2 mail servers running Microsoft Windows Server 2008 R2 and Microsoft Exchange 2010*
- 2 database servers running Microsoft Windows Server 2008 R2 and Microsoft SQL 2008 R2*
- 2 application servers running Windows Server 2008 R2*
- 2 internal web servers running Windows Server 2008 R2*
- 2 external web servers (placed in the DMZ) running Windows Server 2008 R2*
- 1 internal DHCP server running Windows Server 2008 R2*
- 2 file servers running Windows Server 2008 R2, Windows Server 2012, and Windows Server 2012 R2*
- 2 print servers running Windows Server 2008 R2*

* A virtual server running on Windows Server 2012 R2 Hyper-V

External DNS is hosted by a web service.

NETWORK

The three buildings are connected together using 1 Gbps links. Building A has the primary Internet connection, which runs at 100 Mbps. The following sites are connected to the corporate office using a 100 Mbps circuit:

- Detroit
- Miami
- Dallas
- Pittsburgh
- Phoenix
- Seattle
- Oklahoma City
- Portland
- Cleveland
- Reno
- Austin
- Albany
- Denver

The sales/consultant offices are connected to the corporate office with 6 Mbps links.

The sites are connected using Cisco routers and firewalls.

MAINTENANCE WINDOW

The call center must be able to assist customers 24/7. In addition, all external websites must be available 24/7. Maintenance and other tasks can be performed only after coordinating with all stakeholders. The designated maintenance period for production systems is Saturday night. However, because some services or applications cannot be down, you may need to stage the application so that the service or application is functional. In addition, based on the needs of the various departments, systems sometimes cannot be taken down during the normal maintenance period.

70-414 LAB ENVIRONMENT OVERVIEW

The lab environment consists of single domain:

- Contoso.com

The primary servers are in the Contoso.com domain consisting of:

- RWDC01 – Domain Controller, DNS, and WSUS
- Server01 – NLB Cluster node, Configuration Manager, Virtual Machine Manager, Root Certificate Authority, and AD FS
- Server02 – NLB Cluster node, Operations Manager, Subordinate Certificate Authority, and AD RMS
- Server03 – SQL Server Storage Server, DPM, and Web Application Proxy Server
- VServer01 – Failover Cluster Node, and Hyper-V Host
- VServer02 – Failover Cluster Node, and Hyper-V Host

For some of the later labs, you will be using the Adatum.com domain.

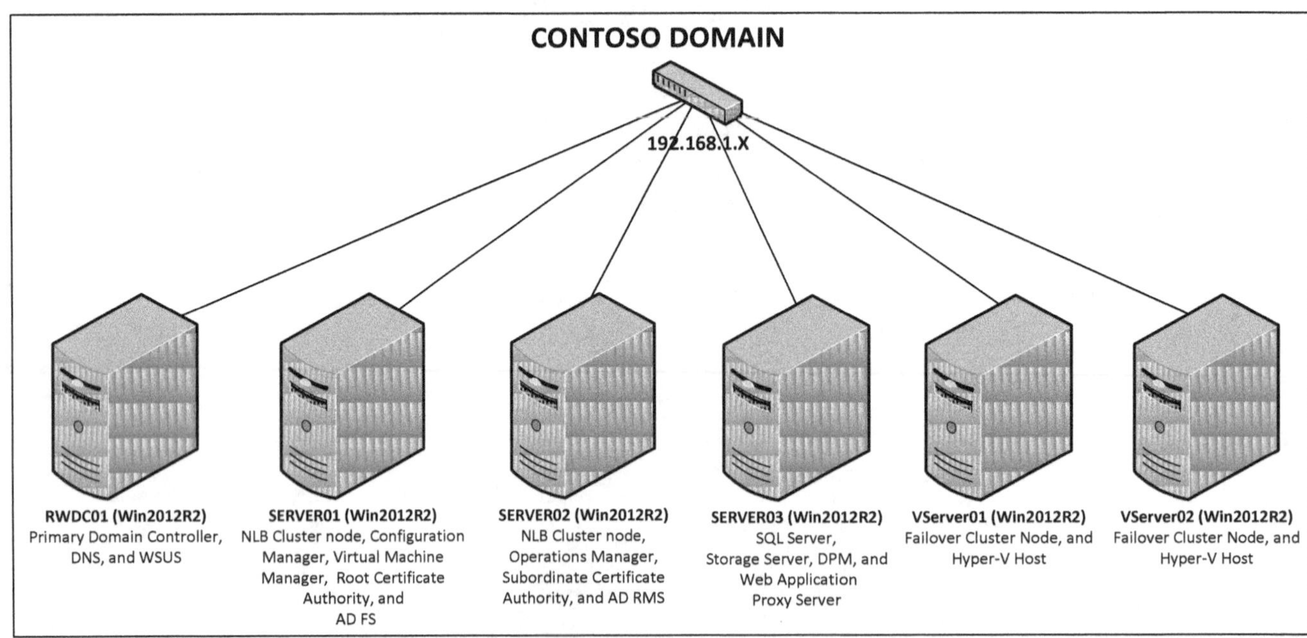

Printed in the USA
K00791SCI080715 01S29053000000000608